MURDE_
& CRIME

NORTHUMBERLAND

MURDER & CRIME

NORTHUMBERLAND

PAUL HESLOP

The
History
Press

To Matty and Annie, my parents.

First published 2011

The History Press
The Mill, Brimscombe Port
Stroud, Gloucestershire, GL5 2QG
www.thehistorypress.co.uk

© Paul Heslop, 2011

The right of Paul Heslop to be identified as the Author
of this work has been asserted in accordance with the
Copyrights, Designs and Patents Act 1988.

ISBN 978 0 7524 5872 4

Typesetting and origination by The History Press
Printed in Great Britain

CONTENTS

ACKNOWLEDGEMENTS

The author wishes to thank staff at Local Studies sections at the following libraries: Newcastle upon Tyne Central Library, North Shields Central Library, and libraries at Berwick, Alnwick, Bedlington, Morpeth, Whitley Bay and Hexham, who assisted with the research required to produce this book, and also staff at Berwick-upon-Tweed Record Office.

Thanks also to Andrew Clark and George Nairn for permission to reproduce images in Chapter 9, Mr John Reed of Bedlington for permission to reproduce the photographs in Chapter 11, and to *Newcastle Evening Chronicle* for permission to reproduce the photographs in Chapters 14 and 15. Special thanks also to my former colleague in Newcastle upon Tyne CID, Alan Oliver, for writing the foreword to my book; and, not least, to my wife, Kathryn, for tolerating my absences caused by research, the need to provide photographs and to write this book.

Please note that in exceptional circumstances some images have been reproduced without sanction of the original publisher, but only after exhausting all means of tracing and identifying them.

FOREWORD

Paul Heslop returns to two of his favourite topics – crime and the county of Northumberland.

This book develops many of the themes from his earlier works. He establishes the facts from historical sources and follows the trial process to the ultimate conclusion, often a death sentence. Was this justice? Ultimately, yes, set against the standards and values of the times.

Details of the investigation are drawn from historical accounts. The trial process and verdicts are a matter of public record. But how can we know the underlying background? The tendency in many books on this subject is to compare historic events with present-day practices and investigative techniques. Paul is well aware that such comparison is futile. The law was different then; modern techniques were either unknown or in their early development; suspects had minimal rights and were sometimes not legally represented when on trial for the most serious of crimes. The words of the legal historian, Stephen, that, 'most persons accused of crime are poor, stupid or helpless', written in 1883, effectively sum up the balance within the criminal justice system for much of the timescale encompassed in this book.

It is interesting to consider the basic facts of the most heinous crime in the criminal calendar. Equally, it is interesting to set the circumstances against the social history of the events. The impact of murder on society is, and probably always has been, one of shock, horror and fascination.

In the writing of this book, Paul Heslop uses his experience as a major crime investigator, gleaned in a career spanning over thirty years in the Northumbria and Hertfordshire police forces. His research is meticulous, and his interpretation of crime and punishment draws the reader into an understanding of the cold and ultimately sad world of criminal investigation.

Alan Oliver, 2011
Former Deputy Chief Constable, Northumbria Police

ABOUT THE AUTHOR

Paul Heslop joined Newcastle upon Tyne City Police in 1965 (later amalgamated into Northumbria Police). He served his time on the beat, supervised by patrol sergeants and inspectors, when on-the-street contact with the public was an essential ingredient in policing. Thereafter he spent most of his career as a detective in the Northumbria and Hertfordshire forces, including service in the Regional Crime Squads in both, the latter involving the investigation of serious crime in London and the Home Counties. He retired from the force in 1995, since when he has become an established writer on such diverse subjects as health and safety in the workplace, country walking and local history. He is the author of eight books to date, and has written about crime for newspapers and periodicals. He lives in the Lake District.

One

'THE BENEFIT OF THE DOUBT'

Berwick-upon-Tweed, 1862

Berwick-upon-Tweed is steeped in violent history, and much of its Elizabethan town wall defences stand today, testimony to days gone by. The walls were never attacked militarily, but were witness nevertheless to a cowardly act of violence in 1862.

John Dixon lived at Warkworth but was staying with friends at Murton, near Berwick. He had known Thomas Hamilton for ten years. About 5 p.m. on Saturday, 1 November 1862, Dixon was in Hide Hill, Berwick, when he saw Hamilton in company with twenty-six-year-old William Deans, whom Dixon also knew. Dixon asked Hamilton how he was. 'Fine,' replied Hamilton, who asked Dixon who he was. 'I'm Harry Dixon's son,' Dixon replied. Hamilton asked him to 'set him along the road', but Dixon said he was off, 'to see his brother.' Dixon thought Hamilton had 'had some drink, but could walk fine', and that Deans was sober. Hamilton and Deans went off down the street together, towards the Nag's Head.

They entered the Nag's Head public house, where each had a glass of whisky. At 5.30 p.m., Matthew Young, a merchant, was in nearby Foul Ford, where he encountered Hamilton and Deans, two strangers to him. Deans was leading Hamilton, as if he was drunk. 'You had better set him against the wall,' said Young to Deans, who appeared sober. 'We've not far to go,' said Deans, as the two men headed towards the walls, in the opposite direction to Hamilton's home.

The next time anyone saw Thomas Hamilton was when Ellen Davidson found him on her doorstep about seven o'clock that evening. Ms Davidson lived near the Cow-Port Gate, part of the town walls, with her house on one side of the gateway and her warehouse on the other. At that time, Ms Davidson had occasion to go across to her warehouse. Whilst there, her attention was drawn to a strange sound, like trampling feet, followed by a loud

Berwick town walls. (© Paul Heslop, 2011)

cry of distress, and she turned just in time to see a man falling at the doorstep of her house. At the same time she saw another man run around the corner of the house. She would later describe him as 'little'.

Ms Davidson asked the fallen man what was the matter. Thomas Hamilton, for it was he, now lying on the ground in agony, replied, 'Are you not done with me yet? Let me die where I am. Let me die in peace.' Ms Davidson tried to move him but was unable to do so. Minutes later Ellen Connolly, who lived in nearby Walkergate Lane, saw William Deans running from the direction of Ms Davidson's house. He ran into Mrs Connolly who asked him if anyone was chasing him. Deans said he had been at Holy Island and the bailiffs were after him. 'Keep it dark,' said Deans, 'and I'll give you a good glass,' whereupon he put his hand into his trouser pocket and pulled out a watch. Ms Connolly noticed the watch had a swivel-end and that it had no chain. He then pulled some money from his pocket and laid it on the watch, still in his hand, as though to hide it. They were two-shilling and half-crown pieces. 'Keep it dark,' said Deans, repeating that he would 'give her a glass in the morning'. He went off in the direction of the High Street.

Constable John Carr attended Ms Davidson's house. Hamilton was able to talk, although 'not sensibly'. He could not move. The constable noticed the flap on his trousers was buttoned up wrong. He sent for an omnibus and took him to the infirmary. Dr Fluker attended at 9.30; he found Thomas Hamilton to have sustained two black eyes and an injury to his cheek. There was discolouration in the perineum (between the genitals and anus), although the skin was not broken. He was in great pain. Fluker also found an injury to the spine, which would account for paralysis below the seat of the injury.

William Deans had been seen and identified by at least two people, as being in company with Thomas Hamilton. The following day, Sunday, Deans was brought to Berwick police station, where Superintendent John Anderson charged him with robbing Hamilton of his watch. Deans said he was not guilty. He said he had met Hamilton in the street and they walked down Hide Hill, and went into a public house together where they had two glasses of whisky. When they left they walked up Foul Ford, as Hamilton said he had to meet someone at Miller's Ropery. When they arrived the man was not there, so they went along the walls towards the Lions (an eighteenth-century house that stands atop the walls). The man was waiting, said Deans, who said he left Hamilton with the man and did not see them again.

In hospital with two black eyes and injuries to his back, and paralysed from the waist down, Thomas Hamilton had been robbed of his watch and some two-shilling pieces. His condition was so serious that on 6 November, Henry John Williams, a clerk, together with a magistrate, Dr Kirkwood, went see Hamilton in hospital. The police had good cause to seek this course of action.

'Hearsay' evidence, where one person says something to another but the accused person, in this case William Deans, does not hear it, is generally inadmissible in court. This is because the accused has no opportunity to respond to whatever is said. An exception is evidence of a *dying declaration*, a statement made by a person who is in imminent danger of death, and knows it. Such a declaration must follow lawful procedures: to be made, on oath, in this case to Henry Williams, in the presence of a magistrate and signed by Hamilton, who declared, 'I have no hope of recovering.' Thomas Hamilton went on to make a statement in connection to a charge of robbery against William Deans.

On 4 December, Superintendent Anderson went to see Deans in prison, where he awaited trial at the next assizes for robbery. Deans, now believing, as Hamilton did, that the latter would die as a result of his injuries, then made this statement to Superintendent Anderson (abridged):

I took Hamilton from the public house with the intention of robbing him. I took him on to the Walls along to the magazine where he wanted to ease himself. He had his trousers down. I robbed him of his watch and his money – two two-shilling pieces, one shilling and a sixpence. I helped to button up his trousers. I buttoned them up the wrong way. I left two sixpences and some halfpence in his pocket because I did not like to leave him destitute. I then left him, took the strap off the watch and threw it into Mrs Hood's garden. I went down to the town…and on to the Mound where I hid the watch in a molehill. I went home, but I felt so ill I could only take one cup of tea. I then went to where I left Hamilton. I could not find him. I thought he must have fallen over the Walls. I went round to look for him, towards the flagstaff. I there found him lying. I sat down beside him for nearly half an hour and cried. I did not know what to do with him, but I got him up upon my back. I carried him and threw him down at Mrs Davidson's door so that she or someone would find him. All I said before about Hamilton having to meet a man at Miller's Ropery is false.

This, then, was William Deans's 'confession' – that he had robbed Thomas Hamilton, but not, significantly, that he had caused the terrible injuries he had received. However, at least one part of his statement was false; he had clearly not hidden the stolen watch and money in a molehill – for Ms Connolly saw it in his hand when he fled the scene.

(© Paul Heslop, 2011)

To put Deans' 'confession' to the test, Superintendent Anderson went to the place where he, Deans, said he had found Hamilton lying, and measured the distance to Mrs Davidson's door – the distance Deans said he had carried Hamilton. It was 650 yards, along rugged paths that traversed three ditches, passed through a gate and crossed a stile. Thomas Hamilton weighed twelve stones. It was scarcely believable that Deans could have carried Hamilton for over one-third of a mile in such circumstances.

On 18 December Superintendent Anderson again saw Hamilton in the infirmary. Hamilton told him, 'I am very ill. I am dying. I hope you will come and see me buried.' Hamilton burst into tears and said, 'That clarty Bill Deans has murdered me.' On 20 December Henry Williams, accompanied by Dr Kirkwood, again went to see Hamilton in the infirmary. Hamilton made another statement, saying:

> I have no doubt in my mind that it was Deans who did all the injury to me. Nobody 'fashed' me but Deans. All the injuries that I sustained were received at the time I was robbed. I never was able to stir from the place where I was robbed. I never fell over any wall. I never recollected falling from any height. He fair murdered me off hand. It [the robbery] would be a very short distance from the cottage where I was found.

Thomas Hamilton died of his injuries on 25 December. The post-mortem examination into his death was made by Dr Fluker. His report makes grim reading. Two of the lumbar vertebrae were fractured, and the lumbar vertebrae itself had been displaced forward. Death was due to injury to the spine. The injuries to the perineum and spine might have been suffered at one time or different times. Dr Fluker was a native of Berwick and knew the place where Hamilton allegedly 'fell over' the Walls, and thought it possible his injuries may have been caused by a fall there. The injury to the perineum was more likely to have been caused by a kick, and a blow from the knee may have fractured the spine; but a fall may have caused that injury. A fall did not cause two black eyes.

Fluker said Hamilton had suffered a great deal, and could not have been moved without causing 'great agony'. The pressure on the spinal marrow would have produced immediate paralysis. He said it was possible that the injury to the spine was caused by someone pulling him backwards with a knee pressed against his back.

At the Northumberland Spring Assizes in March 1863, before Justice Keating, William Deans pleaded not guilty to murder. The evidence of Henry Williams, the clerk, was challenged by Mr Foster, for the defence. Clearly, if Foster could render the dying declaration inadmissible, being hearsay, everything Thomas Hamilton had said in the infirmary would be disregarded. The issue taken up by Foster was 'leading questions', that is, questions requiring a 'yes' or 'no', against Thomas Hamilton speaking freely without being prompted. Williams told the court that Hamilton had said, 'I don't think I shall get better,' which, said Williams, was in answer to his being asked if he had any hope of recovery. There followed a rambling discourse between Mr Foster, the judge and Williams, all of which led to nowhere in particular until Foster declared, 'I submit to your lordship that the dying declaration is not admissible.'

His lordship said: 'In order to admit that declaration I must be satisfied that the man, at the time he made it, was in a dying state. From the evidence I am satisfied that he knew was in a dying state.' The clerk then read Hamilton's declaration, which charged Deans with having inflicted the injuries from which Hamilton felt himself dying. There followed the testimony of Dr Fluker, which, as far as Hamilton's spinal injuries were concerned, was inconclusive; he may have sustained them by Deans forcing his knee against his back, but Fluker could not rule out the possibility they may have been caused by falling from the Walls.

Summing up, his lordship told the jury that Deans' life 'hung upon their verdict'. Deans had robbed Thomas Hamilton, as he now admitted. The question was whether he used the violence that caused his death in order to complete the felony. It was not sufficient that they, the jury, were of the opinion that he offered violence, and *afterwards* Hamilton had met with an accident or with violence, causing his death; they had to be satisfied that the violence that caused his death was the act of the prisoner in the commission of robbing him. 'The prisoner is entitled to the benefit of the doubt,' said his lordship. It was hardly surprising that, after retiring for ten minutes, the jury returned and declared their verdict to be 'not guilty.' 'Thank you gentlemen,' said Deans, obviously relieved.

As he was led away Deans called out, 'The Lord knows I am innocent.' But if he thought he had had the last word he was mistaken, for he was recalled and charged with 'feloniously and violently assaulting Thomas Hamilton and stealing from him a silver watch, value £2, and ten shillings in money'. He was found guilty of robbery with violence. Passing sentence, his lordship saw fit to comment on the first charge, of murder, saying there had been 'sufficient doubt' about how the spinal injury was received, and that Deans had only been saved (from hanging) by the good sense of the jury, who were right to acquit him of murder.

Deans, interrupting, said, 'I would have hung like a man.'

The judge sentenced him to six years penal servitude for robbery.

Deans: 'Thank you, sir, I cannot …' But whatever else he intended to say isn't known, for he was then promptly removed from the dock.

Two

AN UNHAPPY NEW YEAR

Newcastle, 1863

New Year has always been celebrated in the North East of England, a time for consuming alcohol and partying, as we say today. Central Newcastle was as good a place as any to drink and make merry, as Henry Branscomb and lots of others did on New Year's Eve, 1862. It was between one and two o'clock on New Year's morning in Stowell Street – Newcastle's Chinatown today – that Branscomb saw a man dragging a woman out of a passageway. The man had hold of the woman's hair and her arm, and Branscomb saw him strike her three times in the ribs.

Branscomb was joined by William Gillespie and John Buckham, who had been in Darn Crook, now known as St Andrew's Street, and a young boy, John Nesbitt. The party followed the man and woman into nearby West Walls, the narrow lane that runs between the back of Stowell Street and the remains of the old town wall, which still stands as part of Newcastle's historic past. There they bore witness to the woman crying 'Murder!' as her assailant, in the narrow confines of the lane, thrust her to the ground and began to beat her relentlessly. 'What are you striking the woman for?' demanded Branscomb. The man told him to shut up or he would kick him.

William Gillespie said he would go for a policeman, but wilted under the threat of violence from the man who, in the presence of the onlookers, then raped the woman on the muddy ground before tearing her clothes off, including her shoes and stockings and her bonnet. Only when he had finished did the watching party leave the scene, none of them stepping forward to help a victim of crime in that dark lane, a crime they witnessed as rape but, as it would turn out, was also murder.

John Docherty, a tailor, lived with his wife, Margaret, in Buckingham Street, Newcastle. On the morning of Wednesday 31 December he left home at nine o'clock to go to work.

His wife, Margaret, called in the afternoon with his tea, and again around 7.30 p.m. when he gave her three shillings, probably to buy a drink that evening, the celebrated New Year's Eve. Docherty left work at 8.30 p.m. and went for 'a pint or two of beer' to Blakey's Bar in the Adelaide Hotel.

Docherty stayed at Blakey's until after eleven o'clock, by which time we may assume he would have consumed more than a pint or two. In any event, about twenty minutes before he left he was joined by Margaret, and the pair left together around 11.30 p.m. They walked up Gallowgate in the direction of their home in Buckingham Street, about half a mile away. But if John Docherty had had enough alcohol, his wife had not, for she told him that she would have some more and proceeded to enter a public house called Ireland's. Her husband, however, had other ideas, for he grabbed her shoulders and dragged her from the doorway. At that point he was struck on the head and knocked to the ground by one of three men who were standing close by.

Docherty got to his feet and proceeded to walk home. It seems he thought his wife was following behind. Maybe he was too drunk to notice or care, but Margaret was not following him home. In fact, the next time John Docherty saw his wife was in the 'Dead House', as he called it at a court hearing; Margaret Docherty was the very woman dragged by an unknown assailant into West Walls, where she was raped and murdered.

George Storey, a labourer, was another man abroad at New Year, when he met with 'two or three chaps' in Stowell Street. At about two o'clock in the morning he made his way to a house in Buckingham Street, where he saw a man he knew as 'Brassy' who was standing against the table, wearing a cap, 'the same as if he had just come in'. Storey was accompanied by two men, William Spencer and Matthew Connor, no doubt doing their 'first-footings' in keeping with tradition. When, after ten minutes or so, Storey, Spencer and Connor left the house, Brassy followed them. Taking Storey's arm, Brassy said, 'Come along the back Walls, there's a woman there.' The four men went to West Walls and about forty yards along the lane came upon a woman lying on the ground. Storey pulled her shawl aside and saw her face was covered in blood. He took hold of her hand to try and

The West Walls, Newcastle.
(© Paul Heslop, 2011)

help her up, and 'pulled her round a bit' before declaring to the others, 'This woman's dead.' He saw that some of the woman's clothing was strewn about, 'as if they had been torn right off her'. He told Spencer and Connor to go for a policeman.

Brassy told Storey he had been fighting and that his hands were covered in blood. 'You had better go and get your hands washed if you've been fighting,' said Storey, who didn't consider Brassy to be drunk, and evidently didn't consider either that he might be responsible for the woman's injuries. Brassy walked off in the direction of Darn Crook. Storey walked along the lane and encountered Spencer and Connor in Stowell Street. They told him they could not find a policeman, so the three men went to Wardles public house where they had 'gills apiece'. There they encountered two men, Thomas Archbold and John Shearer, who said they would look for a policeman after they had finished drinking their beer. The lack of action by the men in Newcastle town centre was far from commendable, even if they were probably all the worse for liquor.

It may be that word had spread about the woman lying in West Walls, for other men visited the spot where she lay. They were Joseph Parker, Robert Gordon and Thomas Tate. Tate saw Brassy at the scene, and told him he should accompany him in a search for a policeman, but Brassy walked off, saying 'what a shame and a sin it was whoever had done it.' Finally, at about 3.30 a.m., Joseph Parker found a policeman in Newgate Street. Constable William Tate went directly to West Walls where he saw the body of Margaret Docherty: 'Her breast was bare, her legs covered with dirt, her face besmeared with blood,' he told magistrates at a subsequent hearing. PC Tate found her stockings and cap thirty yards away, and saw blood 'lying about', as if a struggle had taken place. He had the body taken to the police station.

Sergeant Thomas Watson visited the scene later that night, finding, among other things, an apron, 'saturated with blood,' and the deceased woman's shoes, each lying on opposite sides of the lane. He also found some pieces of the woman's dress. He had 'an impression that something had been dragged along the ground, and that a desperate struggle had taken place, with blood mixed up with wet mud'.

It wouldn't have taken the police long to identify a likely suspect: 'Brassy' was George Vass, aged nineteen years. On the morning of Friday 2 January, he was arrested at his home by Inspector Thomas Scott, to whom Vass stated: 'About two o'clock I left my father's house in Stowell Street. I met a young man and went along the West Walls and observed a female lying on the ground. I fell over her. I then got up and went for a policeman.' Inspector Scott found that Vass's coat and trousers were bloodstained, and Vass was unable to explain why.

The coat worn by Vass at New Year was handed to Septimus Rayne, the police surgeon. Rayne confirmed the presence of blood on the sleeve, although he could not confirm it was human. On 2 January, Rayne conducted a post-mortem examination on the deceased woman, whom he estimated as fifty years of age. He found her face 'matted with blood and dirt' and 'completely disfigured, with the nose flattened'. Her body was 'begrimed' with dirt, especially her hands, thighs and buttocks. He concluded that 'great violence' had been inflicted upon her, and that she had died as a result of any one of a number of blows. Strangely, he considered she'd had little to drink: 'The stomach was nearly empty, there was only a little dark fluid in it.' He considered the body was lying more or less where the injuries had been inflicted, although she may have crawled a short distance, and that her injuries were inflicted by someone's fists, not by an instrument.

Margaret Docherty's assailant had been seen attacking her, and even raping her, by several men, who, even in darkness, may have remembered his face, especially those who had followed him into the lane. It seems no one was asked to formally identify Vass as that man, but he was charged with murder and placed before the magistrates. Not surprisingly, there were plenty who wanted to watch the proceedings. The *Newcastle Guardian* reported that 'as soon as the door of the court was thrown open a rush was made and the room would have been speedily crammed to suffocation if the police had not taken the precaution to close the door … Several times in the course of the examination of the witnesses the audience gave vent to their feelings in low murmurs as the shocking and disgusting details of the crime were disclosed'. Vass was committed for trial for wilful murder.

George Vass stood trial at the Moot Hall in February. Baron Martin presided. In a faint voice, Vass pleaded 'not guilty' to the charge of murder. Mr Seymour prosecuted but no one, until that morning, had been appointed to defend the prisoner. Mr Blackwell, belatedly appointed to act for Vass, was obliged to apply to his lordship for time to 'get up' a defence, to which the judge agreed 'with an understanding that he would be ready in the course of the day'. When, at last, proceedings got under way, Mr Seymour outlined the facts to the jury before calling witnesses to prove the case. Little of what they said was

St Andrew's Church. Reputedly the oldest church in Newcastle, some murderers were interred in its churchyard after execution. They may have included George Vass. If so, he lies just yards from the crime for which he was convicted in nearby West Walls. (© Paul Heslop, 2011)

challenged by Mr Blackwell, who, at the conclusion of the prosecution's case addressed the jury in his endeavours to persuade them to return a not guilty verdict.

The prosecution, said Mr Blackwell, had brought forward 'a certain class of witnesses' who spoke of a case of rape against the prisoner but not of murder. He 'admitted' that rape had been committed, 'but none of the witnesses spoke of any violence sufficient to cause the injuries described ... There could not have been any motive [to commit murder], for the prisoner had gratified his lust.' He suggested that someone else been the cause of Mrs Docherty's death, 'supposing that a murder had been committed at all,' he said, before adding that 'It was most likely that a carriage had passed over her, as the bruises on her face and the back part of the head would indicate that such might have been done by a carriage wheel, and the other injuries by the hooves of the horses.'

The judge, summing up, thought the 'carriage wheel' defence improbable. The jury agreed, taking but ten minutes to return their verdict: guilty (notwithstanding the evidence of the 'certain class of witnesses'). His lordship's opinion was that after raping Mrs Docherty, Vass 'had by some state of human mind that one could not well define, taken his victim and treated her in a most barbarous and cruel manner'. He committed him to the mercy of the Most High and pronounced sentence of death in the 'usual form'.

Vass, who had 'manifested a certain indifference to all that was going on', appeared unaffected by news of the grim fate that now awaited him. Indeed he had 'chatted and laughed' with another prisoner, Patrick Manion, who was charged with rape and assault, also committed at New Year, and for which he was sentenced to penal servitude for life. Distraught, Manion collapsed in the box, exclaiming, 'Oh my poor mother. I'll never see her more.' Vass, in contrast, maintained his indifference as he was taken down.

The grim fortress of Newgate Gaol having been demolished in 1823, a new prison opened in Carliol Square, Newcastle, in 1828. On Saturday, 14 March 1863 a crowd of over 5,000 gathered to witness justice being carried out. It included many young boys and women, evidently of the 'lowest class ... not being a single respectable face among them', the *Newcastle Guardian* reported. The scaffold was erected at the south-west corner of the gaol, facing the Royal Arcade, the only portion visible to spectators being two upright posts with a cross-beam to which a rope was attached, 'dangling in the air, soon to strangle its victim'. There was a 'truly terrific' crush in the lanes near to the prison, and the shrieks of women and children were heartrending as many were trodden underfoot and had to be rescued in what turned out to be life and death struggles.

Inside the prison, George Vass breakfasted on toast and coffee. The 'miserable youth' acknowledged the justice of his sentence to the chaplain, adding that he was 'not nervous but full of joy at the prospect of being with his Saviour forever'. Even as he spoke, the noise from the crowd outside infiltrated through the thick prison walls.

The hangman was Thomas Askerne. A tremendous shout went up from the crowd as Vass climbed the steps to the scaffold. Vass looked on with a sort of 'dreamy stare' as the faces of thousands of people peered up at him. Those gathered on the scaffold, including Vass, knelt down whilst the chaplain said the Lord's Prayer, and when Vass stood up again he was placed under the 'fateful beam'. A white cap was pulled over his head, the rope adjusted around his neck and his ankles were bound. Then Askerne stepped forward and 'touched a spring', whereupon Vass fell 'and was in an instant swinging in the air'.

Vass never formally admitted to the crime of murder and it has to be said there was a lacking in conclusive evidence to prove he murdered Margaret Docherty. The question of identification arises; just how certain were those who said it was he who murdered a woman in the narrow and darkened confines of West Walls? There was no forensic evidence, as there couldn't be in times when science, such as it was, could not positively identify blood as human, let alone belonging to a particular individual.

Vass, of his own volition, led others to the body. He said he had come across it, and had stumbled over it without knowing it was there. A plausible explanation; there were lots of men, fuelled by alcohol, parading the streets in Newcastle town centre that night. This could account for his clothing being bloodstained. As to counsel suggesting Margaret Docherty had been run over by a horse and carriage, this was no more than speculation, given that no evidence was given to suggest this was the case. Who, in any event, would have driven a horse and carriage along the narrow and darkened West Walls around midnight at New Year? The lane merely leads from its entrance at Darn Crook to an exit a couple of hundred yards further away, with nothing save blank walls in between. Vass admitted raping Margaret Docherty, which was a far cry from 'stumbling' on his victim, so perhaps this does push the likelihood of a safe conviction a step closer, though not conclusively. Rape, itself a capital crime until 1861, was no longer punishable by death.

Justice was not seen to be done in this case. There was not time to put up a proper, coherent defence of Vass, just enough for few quick words. The defence, through no fault of its own, was a shambles, an indictment on a system where someone was standing trial for his life. Even if George Vass was guilty of murder, under a system like this how many others who were convicted were not guilty?

No one sought a reprieve for Vass, who might otherwise have been transported. 'Not the slightest effort was made in any quarter to obtain a mitigation of the extreme penalty of the law ... Even those who were opposed to all capital punishment were silent'. Public executions were regarded as a rightful expectation to witness justice being carried out, but this was the last public execution in Newcastle upon Tyne. Given the disgraceful and life-threatening scenes enacted outside the prison that day, it was just as well.

Three

'WITH SLIGHT PROVOCATION'

Dinnington, 1875

They were young men who, like so many others in south-east Northumberland, worked down the pit in grim conditions. Who could blame them when, on a fine winter's day, they set out to enjoy some fresh, country air and exercise their right to go shooting on snow-covered fields? They were George Hunter, twenty-three, Thomas Arnott and Robert Scouler, all of whom were armed with shotguns, and twenty-year-old William Wood. Gun ownership was commonplace in Victorian England, and shooting birds an acceptable practice. But a day out, followed by a few drinks in the pub, ended in tragedy, with Dinnington still getting over the shock of Richard Charlton murdering his wife and shooting her sister barely six months before.

It was 2 p.m. on Thursday 9 December when the four coal miners walked the mile and a half from Dinnington to Prestwick Lodge where they shot randomly at birds. As Arnott would later say, 'We were not very particular.' They occupied themselves thus until around five o'clock, when it began to get dark, then walked back to the village where three of them entered the Carr Gate public house, now the Swan. Robert Scouler, being teetotal, went next door to Mrs Johnston's house.

Hunter, Arnott and Wood met two other local men in the pub, Samson Mead and Thomas Thorn. They all drank together, enjoying one another's company, 'with no high words between them', until Scouler came in about 8.30 p.m. to enquire whether his companions were ready to go home yet. They weren't, so Scouler loaded his gun and went outside to shoot rabbits. When he returned, at about 9.40, all five men left the pub to walk to their homes.

They walked together at first, towards the centre of the village. Wood was throwing snowballs, striking Thorn at least once, causing no ill-feeling through what, after all, is a common-place prank. They encountered George Stoker, a local schoolteacher, who presented them with a petition, drawn up on behalf of Richard Charlton so that his sentence of death would be commuted to life imprisonment. They all signed. Further along the road Thorn left the group to go to his house, followed by Mead.

Arnott and Scouler walked ahead of Hunter and Wood, the distance between the two pairs being about 100 yards. One might picture the scene that night: darkness, unlit streets, but perhaps some light from the moon reflecting off a carpet of snow; and silence, but with night-time sounds occasionally reverberating in the darkness. Sound certainly carried to Arnott and Scouler, who distinctly heard George Hunter say to Wood, 'If you don't stop clotting or heaving I will fire.' They heard Wood reply, 'Oh, you will not fire at me Geordie.' Arnott and Scouler weren't the only ones to hear Hunter's voice. Christopher MacDougal, local molecatcher, had left his house and seen Thorn, then Mead, leave the group, then heard someone say, 'Take a shot,' followed by, 'Geordie you are not going to fire,' although he could neither see nor tell who said it. In any event, after a few moments, Arnott, Scouler and MacDougal heard the distinctive sound of a gunshot.

None of them at that time could see either Hunter or Wood due to a bend in the road. But a minute or two later Hunter hurried up to Arnott and Scouler, and addressed the former, saying, 'Let's have your flask, Tom,' meaning his flask of powder used for loading his gun. Arnott handed him his flask, and enquired, 'What have you fired at, Geordie?' ' I have fired at Willie,' Hunter replied.

'You don't mean to say you have fired at Willie, Geordie,' said Arnott, repeating the words Hunter had just said to him.

'I have, Tom,' said Hunter.

'Have you hit him?' asked Arnott.

'Yes,' said Hunter.

The Swan, Dinnington,
formerly the Carr Gate Inn.
(© Paul Heslop, 2011)

Arnott, Scouler and MacDougal, ran to where William Wood was now lying in the snow, face downwards near the hedge by the church. Arnott put his arms around him, and said, 'Are you hurt, Willie?' But Willie did not answer him, as he lay with blood oozing from his chest into the snow. Arnott and Scouler ran to Mead's house. Mead too had heard the shot. He and his wife then went to the house of Thomas Thorn, and thence to find a policeman. Soon after, Arnott and Mead returned to the scene, to find Wood lying in a pool of blood and Hunter lying on the ground beside him, his gun leaning against the hedge. Arnott picked the gun up and handed it to Mead, saying, 'Keep that gun, Sam, until somebody comes.'

Meanwhile Robert Scouler had gone to Seaton Burn to fetch Doctor Allan Walker, who attended the scene at 10.30. Walker saw that William Wood was dead. Shortly afterwards, Police Constable William Davidson arrived. George Hunter was still lying on the footpath. Samson Mead gave the policeman Hunter's gun, which he saw was at full cock but not loaded, and was later found to have no powder in it. He put his finger into the muzzle and found it black and damp, suggesting it had been recently fired. The body of William Wood was taken to the Bay Horse public house. PC Davidson told Hunter to get up, but he refused to stand, so Arnott and the constable picked him up and 'trailed' him to the police house. Hunter would not speak to the officer, who took him to the Moot Hall, Newcastle, the same night. When PC Davidson charged him with shooting William Wood, he replied, 'I cannot mind anything about it.'

There is no doubt that William Wood had been shot at close range by a shotgun. Dr Walker, testifying at the inquest at the Bay Horse, said he saw holes in Wood's jacket over the left breast, and when opening the jacket he saw a 'very large hole', about four inches in circumference, in the left shoulder of the jacket and shirt. He then saw 'a great many' shot-holes on the anterior and upper part of the chest. He made a post-mortem examination the following day, finding a bruise on the side of the forehead and another on the nose. These, he concluded, were consistent with a fall. There were about a dozen shot-holes on the left shoulder, and the shoulder joint was completely smashed with the bones protruding. The upper part of the chest was riddled with shot. Dr Walker thought Wood had been shot from a distance of 5 to 10 yards, and that he was probably in a stooping position at the time.

One wonders how much, if any, of the events that night were caused through or influenced by the alcohol consumed in the Carr Gate public house by all those concerned, save Scouler. Thomas Arnott said 'we had a few pints between us' and that he and Wood had a glass of whisky between them. Arnott thought they had had 'eight pints of beer,' meaning himself, Mead and Thorn. He did not allude to the amount of alcohol Hunter and Wood consumed, but was adamant that he, Hunter and Wood were all 'sober enough'. Ruth Bell, licensee of the Carr Gate, told the inquest that Arnott and Wood and another man whom she did not apparently know – George Hunter, presumably – were in the tap room and were supplied with pints of beer. She was 'in and out' so could not say how much. She stated there was 'no quarrelling' between them, and added that William Wood at one point 'was outside pelting snow'. All the men were 'quite sober' when they left, she said.

George Hunter appeared before Baron Bramwell at the Northumberland Spring Assizes at the Moot Hall, Newcastle, charged with murdering William Wood. The facts of the case were straightforward enough, but for the prosecution Mr Greenhow told the jury they had to consider whether Hunter fired the gun intentionally or accidentally. The gun was fired immediately after a threat to fire, he said, and Hunter had never stated he fired it accidentally. Surely if he had fired accidentally he would have given some sort of explanation, Mr Greenhow added that the charge of murder could only be reduced to manslaughter if there had been some provocation or excuse. The deceased man had been stooping when he was shot, in the act of gathering snowballs perhaps. But throwing snowballs, he suggested, was not sufficient provocation for doing such a deadly act, and Hunter had not been in any danger himself.

Mr Blackwell, defending, said this was a 'painful case'. The deceased man and Hunter had been friends, and there was no premeditation on Hunter's part to take his friend's life. He would not suggest that Hunter was drunk, but he had had a drink and under the influence of drink he may have forgotten his gun was loaded. He might have thought it was not loaded at all. It was well known that *men of the prisoner's class* carried guns carelessly, even when loaded, and the gun might have gone off accidentally. If the jury had reasonable doubt, then they must acquit Hunter of the charge.

It was a sad case, said the judge. On the one hand it seemed shocking that the prisoner should undergo severe punishment if he was convicted of murder or manslaughter. He might lose his life. But the jury had to bear in mind 'that it was necessary that people should be restrained from the exercise of violent and ferocious passion which caused mischief and death to others.' A person who was in no danger of repeating an offence of this sort should be punished in order to deter others. The jury had a duty: if the evidence showed George Hunter was guilty of murder they must say so.

William Wood's grave, Dinnington churchyard. (© Paul Heslop, 2011)

The fact was, said his lordship, George Hunter shot William Wood. If he wilfully aimed and fired he was guilty of murder. Premeditation was not necessary. If the jury thought he did not shoot Wood by accident they must say so. There was a threat, which proved he knew the gun was loaded and it was fired immediately afterwards. After he had shot him Hunter ran to his companions, telling them he had fired and hit him and asked for Arnott's powder flask. He had never said it was an accident, nor expressed any regret. He concluded by saying that if the gun went off through carelessness on Hunter's part he was guilty of manslaughter.

The jury took three-quarters of an hour to find George Hunter guilty of murder, 'with a strong recommendation to mercy on account of his previous good character and the slight provocation he had received'. The judge noted this, telling Hunter the jury 'could find no other verdict'. He sentenced him to death. Hunter was taken to the county gaol at Morpeth. In the meantime a petition was sent to Queen Victoria, 'praying for a commutation of sentence of death', and reports were asked for by the Home Secretary. These proved to be unfavourable as far as Hunter's previous 'good character' was concerned, for it was shown that he had twice previously shot at people, and only a few days before he shot William Wood had threatened a man with whom he had quarrelled with a gun. The Home Secretary saw no reason for recommending the royal prerogative of mercy to the Queen.

At 7.45 a.m. on 28 March 1876, the prison bell at Morpeth Gaol tolled, and at 7.48 the prison governor, Lieutenant Wookey, shook hands with Hunter and handed him over to the custody of the sheriff. Hunter was taken to the scaffold and hanged by William Marwood. At the very moment the bolt was released and the 'unhappy man struggled in the throes of death', the black flag was run up above the prison walls to signify that the execution had taken place.

It interesting to note defence counsel's remark, that 'men of George Hunter's class carried guns carelessly'. This, by implication, meant that a member of say, the aristocracy, would never be so careless. Whilst noting that counsel's remarks were utter nonsense, he said them in his endeavour to have his client acquitted. As to the crime, one cannot help but wonder what George Hunter was thinking when he shot his friend. Even allowing for the presence of alcohol in his body, however much, there cannot have been any logical reason for his actions, certainly not for being hit by a few snowballs. The answer, surely, is that men should not carry guns. Sadly, in Victorian times, many did so routinely.

Four

A WICKED CONSPIRACY

Edlingham, 1879

It was a moonlit night. Ideal for those who would be up to mischief. Poachers, especially. But at Edlingham, a few miles from Alnwick, there would surely be nought to interrupt the peace that was enjoyed by the Revd Matthew Buckle, vicar of the parish, and his daughter, Georgina, sleeping soundly in the vicarage in what was, and still remains, an isolated community, barely large enough to be described as a village.

But at one o'clock on that Friday morning, 7 February, that peace was interrupted when Miss Buckle was awakened by a noise downstairs. She was certain there was a noise, for she went to the top of the stairs, stamped her foot and called out, 'Who is there?' No reply came, so she went to her father's bedroom where she awakened him and told him what she had heard.

The reverend did not hesitate. Getting from his bed he told his daughter he would go downstairs to investigate. Her pleas not to were ignored as Buckle pulled on his dressing gown, lit a candle and proceeded to go downstairs, taking with him on old sword. He was brave, if foolhardy, as was his daughter, who went with him.

There were two men. Buckle pressed his sword against the body of one of them; he would later say he thought, wrongly, that he had wounded him. The man held what appeared to be an iron bar – because, as Buckle believed, 'burglars seldom carry guns'. In the darkness, Miss Buckle tackled the other man, grabbing him by the hair, but he wriggled free. The candle went out, then there was a shot, discharged from the shotgun held by the man the Buckle had tackled. The charge struck the wooden door, splintering it, before ricocheting into the wall opposite. The shot struck Buckle's shoulder, and tore his gown.

'Are you hit, papa?' asked Georgina. 'Merely grazed,' replied her father, before backing from the room to the staircase. He made to enter the room again, only to be pinioned by his daughter in an attempt to restrain him. Even as she held on to him, Buckle heard the man

Edlingham vicarage. (© Paul Heslop, 2011)

ramming down a second charge, being given time to re-load thanks to his daughter's well-intentioned actions. The Buckles hastened upstairs then, and the intruders fled.

After half an hour the Buckles went back downstairs, now accompanied by their elderly cook, Jane Brown. Mrs Brown picked up a chisel, which she handed to Buckle. The drawing room had been ransacked, the door 'violently broken open'. Evidently the men had entered by forcing the hasp on the window with the chisel. One item had been stolen: Georgina's watch, which had been left on the mantelpiece. It was a ladies' watch with a gold face, 'slightly filigreed'. The watch was attached to an 'ordinary dog chain', ten or twelve inches long with an albert bar.

Later that morning, a farm manager, William Sanderson, went to the vicarage and searched a stable where he found two impressions on some hay, 'as if two people had been sitting there'. He then went to the dining room where, about a foot from the door, he found a scrap of newspaper, which he later handed to Superintendent Harkes, the policeman in charge. The chisel was also handed to the police.

Shortly after 5 a.m., Dr Wilson went to the vicarage where he examined the Buckles. The Revd Buckle has suffered a gunshot wound to the shoulder; his daughter had been struck by one pellet. Neither was seriously injured.

The police lost no time in identifying the likely culprits. Michael Brannagan, aged forty-four, and Peter Murphy, twenty-two, were known poachers and had been seen often enough out on the moors about Alnwick. Inspector Harrison and another policeman were at Brannagan's house in Alnwick before 5 a.m., but he was not at home. They went next

Intruders disturbed – the dramatic scene in the vicarage. (Author's collection)

door to Murphy's house, but he was not at home either. Just after seven o'clock the police returned to Brannagan's, where they found him inside pulling his trousers off. When asked where he had been through the night, Brannagan replied, 'You want information but you will not get it here.' His coat, corduroy trousers and clogs were all wet.

When the police were in Brannagan's house, Murphy turned up. 'What's up?' he enquired. Inspector Harrison went with Murphy into his house, where he found his wet clothes drying by the fire. Murphy lived with his sister and her husband, John Redpath. The police showed Redpath the chisel recovered at the vicarage, which he identified as his.

Brannagan and Murphy were charged with 'burglariously breaking into the vicarage', and shooting the Revd Buckle and his daughter with intent to murder. When they appeared before the magistrates, the hearings were held 'behind closed doors' for a reason never explained, and a 'strong case' was reportedly made out against them.

Firstly, there was the evidence of the chisel, recovered at the scene of the crime and identified as his by John Redpath, who lived in the same house as Peter Murphy. Then there was the evidence of Superintendent Harkes, who found the drawing room window and a door had been forced, and the chisel corresponded with the marks made. Outside, he 'observed' two sets of footprints that led through the grounds to the main road. Both prisoners said they had been 'out' at Charlton Moor that night, meaning they had been poaching. Neither admitted to breaking into the vicarage.

Harkes said that when he took the prisoners' boots and clogs to the vicarage they corresponded with the footprints found there. He took two plaster-casts of the clogs and two on the boots the next day, which he produced at court. He had searched Murphy's jacket but found nothing of significance. This speedy and successful result merited praise from the Revd Buckle, who wrote to the *Alnwick Mercury*, of the events on the night of the burglary, including his daughter's bravery, 'No daughter could have shown more heroic devotion in seeking to protect her father's life at the price of her own ...' He ended, 'Owing to the energy, promptitude and intelligence with which the police acted under the direction of Mr Harkes, the burglars were in custody within five hours.'

★ ★ ★

Michael Brannagan and Peter Murphy appeared before Justice Manisty at the Northumberland Spring Assizes that April, charged with burglary, and 'unlawfully and feloniously shooting with a certain gun' loaded with powder and leaden shot with intent to murder, whereby bodily injury was inflicted. They denied the charges.

Once again evidence was given, recalling the events at Edlingham vicarage on the night 6-7 February. No evidence was given by John Redpath, however, who was excused when Dr Wilson testified that he was too ill to attend. Redpath's deposition was read out instead, stating that the chisel he had been shown by the police was his and that he had never given Peter Murphy permission to use it.

In addition, Sergeant Isaac Gare told the court that on 4 March, nearly a month after the crime, he had found a piece of cloth and a button outside the vicarage drawing room window. The cloth, he said, fitted into a place in Brannagan's trousers where a piece was missing. When cross-examined about the lapse in time before he found the cloth, he explained that snow had fallen shortly after the burglary, and so the cloth and button had not been found sooner. Sergeant Gare also produced an envelope which he found outside the window, which, he said, bore the impression of hob nails similar to those on the boots of the accused.

One witness not called to testify was Police Constable Sprott, who, after their arrests, accompanied Brannagan and Murphy to Charlton Moor where they admitted they had been poaching, and where they said they had hidden some rabbits they had caught. Sure enough, the rabbits were exactly where they said they had hidden them. Superintendent Harkes evidently decided it was still possible for Brannagan and Murphy to have committed the burglary at Edlingham, even if they had been on Charlton Moor.

Dr Wilson gave evidence of the Buckles' injuries, and of his examination of the prisoners, neither of whom was injured. He told the court that on 16 February he examined Murphy's coat – which had been examined earlier by Superintendent Harkes – and between the lining and one of the pockets he found a piece of newspaper, evidently missed by Harkes, which was placed next to the piece found at the vicarage and found to 'correspond exactly'.

A crucial part of the evidence was the chisel, allegedly identified by John Redpath as his and thus, by implication, taken from the house and used in the burglary. Mr Milvain, defending, sought to show that the chisel did not belong to Redpath at all. Agnes Simm, who used to reside in Redpath's house, was present when the police came to the house on 7 February. She said Redpath was short-sighted and she had never seen him with the chisel. Mary Ann Murphy, Murphy's sister, described Redpath as 'a blind old man'.

Michael Brannagan. (Author's collection)   Peter Murphy. (Author's collection)

Brannagan and Murphy were unable to testify in their own defence, in accordance with the law at that time.

Mr Milvain had much to say to the jury in his closing address, including of the 'extraordinary circumstances' whereby the police had initially failed to find a piece of newspaper in Murphy's jacket, which they had searched, yet a piece matching that found at the scene had been found over week later by Dr Wilson. He added that despite the Revd Buckle lunging at one of the men with his sword, neither was injured, and concluded by saying the evidence against the prisoners was circumstantial, and that there was 'no case to deprive them of their liberty'. The jury, after nearly three hours' deliberation, disagreed, and returned guilty verdicts. The judge had much to say, too, including his assertion that he had 'sought in vain for any redeeming circumstances which would justify him reducing the punishment'. He sentenced each man to penal servitude for life.

★ ★ ★

Seven years passed, in which Messrs Murphy and Brannagan languished in grim Victorian prisons. But if they were out of sight, they were not out of the mind of Mr Charles Percy, an Alnwick solicitor who, in September, 1886, chancing upon the Revd J.M. Perry, vicar of St Paul's Church, Alnwick, asked the good vicar to kindly attend his office.

Raising the case of the Edlingham burglary, Percy told Perry he was in possession of information' which, if true, meant Murphy and Brannagan were the victims of a terrible injustice. Had Perry ever heard of one George Egdell? The reverend had, although only by his poor reputation. Well, said Percy, 'two or three things' had come to his knowledge, which had raised the 'faintest suspicion' that he was connected with the burglary.

Firstly, Egdell's niece, Margaret Mills, had made a statement to Percy, saying that she had been living at her grandmother's, and on the morning of the burglary Egdell's wife came to her grandmother's room about four o'clock saying if the police came and enquired if George had been out all night she was to say 'No'. But Margaret had heard Egdell going upstairs about half an hour before, which meant he had been. The following morning Margaret saw Mrs Egdell again, who said that George and another man 'had been at the Buckles', and the old man had heard them and come downstairs and they had fired a gun. George had borrowed a coat, which he burnt 'for fear the police might come'.

Percy said that a roadman called White, who lived opposite Egdell, had also made a statement, saying that on the morning of the burglary he remembered Egdell 'coming in'. John Allan, the sweep, had stated that Superintendent Harkes had come to his kitchen and said, 'There has been a mistake about the Edlingam affair, but it cannot be recalled now.' Allan told Percy that 'they [Brannagan and Murphy] were the wrong men', and that the 'biggest burglar in Alnwick was George Egdell'.

Percy told Revd Perry that Egdell was now very ill. His wife had hinted that she would not let her husband die without confessing, and Percy implored the vicar to visit Egdell to see 'if there was any truth in it'. Perry agreed to do so, and visited Edgell, whose daughter, Maria, aged eight, had consumption and would not survive. And then, on 16 November 1886, when Egdell visited Perry at St Paul's vicarage, and the good vicar broached the subject of the burglary, Egdell, becoming agitated, replied, 'Oh sir, but I was not the man who fired the shot. But the man who did told me that if he was sure he could not be punished he would confess all.' Perry then summonsed Percy, and in his presence Egdell repeated those words, and asserted that the two men now in prison were innocent. That was as far as Egdell would go; he would not name the other man.

Perry went to see Miss Buckle, who thought that there had not been a miscarriage of justice, but volunteered one piece of information whereby the truth or falsehood of a confession might be tested: her stolen watch and chain had been advertised in the papers, but not a seal that was attached to it, the description of which had never been revealed. If anyone could describe the seal he must be one of the men who stole the watch. The seal, she said, was in the form of a 'little bird', but she bound Perry to secrecy on it. However, a day or so later, when Perry and the solicitor, Mr Percy, went to see her, she refused to answer any questions. Perhaps the presence of a solicitor frightened the good vicar's daughter, but she did tell him that if Percy could find out for himself what the seal looked like she might then believe the wrong men had been convicted.

Bound to secrecy, the reverend could not tell Percy what the seal looked like. Percy thus decided to find it out for himself, which he tried to do for two years, whilst all the time Brannagan and Murphy languished in jail.

And then, on 8 October 1887, Percy went to see Egdell and told him directly that he suspected he was one of the men who burgled the vicarage, and the least he could do was tell the truth on behalf of the wrongly-imprisoned men. Miss Buckle had said there was a peculiarity about the watch and chain and without hesitation Egdell said, 'That would be the gilt eagle [the seal] at the end of the chain.' Egdell went on to describe it in accurate detail, proving he had at least seen it. Percy took this down in writing and showed it to the Revd Perry, who had still not breathed a word of what Miss Buckle had told him. This statement was then sent to the Solicitor for the Treasury – in effect, the Home Office.

Egdell's confession would only be accepted if he withdrew all conditions in making it – his name was not yet divulged – which he declined to do, saying that he had made it on condition that he would not be prosecuted. The Home Office made it clear that his confession could be used in evidence against him and, to his credit, Egdell then voluntarily made a signed confession to being one of the men who committed the burglary at Edlingham vicarage.

Egdell did not name the second man, although Perry had a good idea who this was. But the man, on a second interview with Perry, agreed to confess. He was Charles Richardson, a ne'er-do-well, who had been suspected of shooting and killing Police Constable George Grey at Eglingham, six years earlier. In his confession, Richardson admitted that on the night 6-7 February he and his companion (Egdell) went to the Edlingham district to poach. They caught no game, but in the 'hardness of the time' and having nothing they decided to try and get into the vicarage.

They had previously been in an old shed near the vicarage and found an old poke (sacks), which they tore up in an outhouse at the back of the vicarage, and tied the sacking round their feet with string. They found a chisel in the outhouse, and forced the drawing room widow with it. Inside the vicarage they lit a candle, broke into some drawers and stole some coppers. On the left side of the mantelpiece was a watch hanging up on a triangle. He, Richardson, grabbed it. It was a lady's watch with a gold face. It had a silver chain attached, about a foot long. At one end of the chain was a gold eagle with spread wings.

Then Mr Buckle and his daughter appeared. The vicar came forward with a sword and the shotgun, which Richardson carried, went off accidentally (he said). It was not pointed at Buckle and the shot struck the staircase somewhere. When the Buckles went upstairs he and his accomplice fled, leaving the chisel behind. They crossed the fields and at Mossy Ford he hid the watch in a quarry, together with the gun, gunpowder and shot. He, Richardson, went home and burnt his trousers and boots. At about 4 a.m. two policemen came and asked to see his boots. He showed them a dry pair. Afterwards he went back for the watch, which he wore for several months. Eventually he took it to Newcastle but was unable to sell it so he threw it into the Tyne.

So much for Superintendent Harkes's plaster impressions of boots and clogs matching those at the scene of the crime; so much for the chisel belonging to John Redpath; so much for the matching pieces of newspaper; and so much for Sergeant Gare finding the piece of cloth torn from Brannagan's coat.

On 9 November 1888, in the House of Commons, Mr Milvain, who had defended Brannagan and Murphy at their trial in 1879 but was now a Member of Parliament, said that he would ask the Home Secretary about the case. The confessions of Egdell and Richardson, who were able to describe in detail the gold eagle, was proof enough that they were the guilty men and it was hardly a surprise that Brannagan and Murphy were freed. The identification of the seal was a critical point, allaying suspicion that

Egdell and Richardson weren't lying in order to have criminal associates released from prison.

In November 1888 George Egdell and Charles Richardson appeared before the Alnwick magistrates. Once again witnesses' testimonies were heard, this time including two new witnesses, Michael Brannagan and Peter Murphy. Another 'new' witness was Mr Whinham, a jeweller, of Alnwick Market Place, who said he bought the seal from Charles Richardson in 1882. The seal was damaged, so he sent it away to have it repaired. When he failed to sell the seal he himself wore it, but when he saw the report of the case in the *Gazette* he handed the seal to Mr Brewis Elsdon, who was acting on behalf of the Home Office.

Egdell, now forty-seven, and Richardson, fifty-three, appeared before Baron Pollock at the Northumberland Winter Assizes in December 1888, charged with the burglary, and shooting Revd Buckle and his daughter with intent to commit murder. Mr Seymour represented both men. The prosecution offered no evidence on the shooting charges, 'a very proper course,' said the judge. Egdell and Richardson pleaded guilty to the burglary and awaited their fate whilst Mr Seymour spoke on their behalf.

Seymour had much to say, including that the gun was fired but that Egdell and Richardson had asserted that it went off by accident, hence that charge was withdrawn. Egdell was a married man, said Mr Seymour. If he had been single he would have 'rushed forward' to save Brannagan and Murphy and 'not left them for an hour in prison'; but he had a wife and child whose daily bread was dependent upon him. (One accepts reality can be stretched on occasion by defence counsel giving mitigating circumstances.) Egdell's child, sadly, passed away in 1886, and it was then he was persuaded to confess.

Richardson, said Mr Seymour, could have used the gun, either to shoot the Revd Buckle, or to bludgeon him with it. It had been in his power, but his conscience prompted him to withdraw it (he made no mention of Richardson reloading the gun whilst the Revd Buckle was being restrained by his daughter). Then he referred to a petition, signed by 3,000 people 'of all classes of society', praying for mercy for the accused. Nothing, he said, could 'spare Egdell's suffering these past ten years'. He implored his lordship to be merciful after he had come forward 'to be immolated upon the altar of justice that

Charles Richardson (left) and George Egdell. (Author's collection)

he might save the innocent from their unfortunate doom.' He added that his lordship's sentence would 'fall upon confessed burglars, but it would also fall upon Christian martyrs.' The judge sentenced them to five years imprisonment.

After the trial, in the House of Commons, the Home Secretary, Henry Matthews, confirmed a free pardon had been granted to Brannagan and Murphy and, to cries of 'hear hear', that each man had been awarded £800 compensation. This was a grand sum for two men who had once stolen rabbits to eat, but nothing could satisfactorily compensate for spending nearly ten years in prison for a crime they did not commit. Another issue raised was the 'pressing necessity' for accused persons to be able to give evidence on their own behalf. Had Brannagan and Murphy been able to do so, a grave injustice might have been averted, which brings us to the conduct of the police.

It is clear the police believed that either one of two pairs of men committed the burglary at the Edlingham vicarage. They went first to the homes of Egdell and Richardson, but found their clothing and boots dry; being the real culprits, they knew they had to get rid of incriminating evidence. Then the police called on Brannagan and Murphy, who had been out poaching rabbits that night, and decided it must be they who had committed the crime. Instead of examining the facts objectively, they decided who the burglars were and fashioned the evidence to suit the case.

After the early arrests of Brannagan and Murphy, Revd Buckle had written of 'the energy, promptitude and intelligence' of the police under the direction of Superintendent Harkes. But Harkes, upon whose instigation Dr Wilson searched the jacket and found the piece of newspaper – planted there by the police – was now dead. Four policemen were indicted with conspiracy and appeared before Justice Denman at the Moot Hall, Newcastle. All four argued that the statements of Egdell and Richardson were worthless because they were criminals who were now serving terms of imprisonment. Then the judge killed the prosecution off, saying that the police might have believed they had been honestly endeavouring to do their duty to secure convictions. They were all acquitted. One recoils at the injustice of this.

This was a tragic case. But it could have been worse for the hapless Brannagan and Murphy, for if the Revd Buckle or his daughter had been shot dead that night they would surely have hanged. Not even the diligent efforts of the solicitor, Mr Percy, or the Revd Perry, or indeed the belated confessions of Egdell and Richardson, could have made amends for the actions of those policemen.

A plaque dedicated to the memory of Revd Buckle. (© Paul Heslop, 2011)

Five

A MOST PASSIONATE
AFFECTION

Tynemouth, 1894

It was just before eight o'clock on a summer's evening, and John Davison and Sarah Schofield were sitting on a seat near Holy Saviour's Church, Tynemouth. As they sat there they noticed another young couple walking towards the church. Minutes later, John and Sarah set off in the same direction, and, seeing the couple again, could not fail to notice that this time the young man was walking a few yards ahead with the girl now hurrying after him. When she caught him John and Sarah became witnesses to murder.

First, the young man knocked the girl down. She got to her feet and put her hands around his neck in a gesture of affection, but he turned and struck her again, and this time John and Sarah saw that he held a knife in his hand. Then they saw someone approaching on a tricycle.

It was the Revd Thomas Bold Nichols who, approaching the church, saw the couple on the road, the girl lying face upwards, the young man on top of her. He clearly saw him strike the girl three times, each of the blows aimed at her neck. The young man then turned, saw Nichols and ran off. Nichols leapt from his tricycle and gave chase to her assailant. However, he soon lost sight of his quarry and so returned to the injured girl, who had now got to her feet and was leaning against the churchyard wall 'bleeding horribly' from a wound in her neck and unable to speak. Nichols tried to stop the bleeding with his handkerchief and laid her down on the footpath.

Edward Stacey, a clerk at the station, who was out walking with his mother, also witnessed the attack. He heard the girl shriek and saw the man strike her two or three times on the neck. As the man ran off Stacey gave chase, running to the back of Tynemouth railway station where he lost sight of him. James Gibson, a chemist, out walking with his wife, had seen people running near to the church and shortly after saw Mrs Stacey who called out,

'Stop that man. He is running through the field, round the church.' Gibson ran towards the church and immediately encountered the young man who stopped and faced Gibson, threatening him with a knife, 'the blade protruding about four inches from his clenched fist'. He slashed at Gibson, who later described him as 'very ugly to behold; he had the appearance of a madly desperate man. My wife saw it and it haunts her still.' Gibson avoided the blow offered by the man, who then ran off down a private road leading to the north platform of the railway station before scrambling up the embankment and disappearing over a wall. Stacey and Gibson continued the chase but had to give up when they became exhausted.

The young woman was Mary Marshall, known as Molly, aged seventeen and described as 'fair and good looking'. She lived at Cross Street, Tynemouth, with her parents. PC Hall, receiving early notification of the incident, attended the scene immediately, and had 'six or seven young men' carry Mary into the vestry of the church, where she died a few minutes later. Soon afterwards, her father, Robert Marshall, came to the vestry where he identified the body of his daughter. It was hardly surprising that he was shocked and he left the scene in a dazed condition.

Dr Wilkinson attended the church just as Mary passed away. On examining her, he found two 'large penetrating wounds' in her neck. The upper wound, by the ear, was deep and had opened the windpipe. The other was lower, and the muscles of the neck had been severed; it was so deep that it penetrated to the bones of the shoulder. Mary's hands were cut in her vain attempts to prevent her assailant stabbing her. The doctor had her body removed to the mortuary.

This was a tragic and cold-blooded killing of an innocent girl. But although her assailant had fled, his identity became quickly apparent; he was twenty-year-old Samuel George

Holy Saviour's Church, Tynemouth. (© Paul Heslop, 2011)

Emery, a private in the South Staffordshire Regiment. Having fled the scene of the crime, he went to the Crescent Tavern, Hudson Street, Tynemouth, where he ordered whisky and cheese, apparently unconcerned about the wicked deed he had perpetrated.

★ ★ ★

Samuel Emery was a native of West Bromwich. Until about three weeks previously his regiment had been stationed at the barracks in Tynemouth Castle. For three months he had courted Mary and when his regiment had been transferred to Strenshall, near York, they had communicated by letter. One of Emery's letters showed that he had received correspondence from an unknown person, possibly a rival for Mary's affections, which prompted him to write to her on 13 July, saying (abridged):

> I have had a letter from a friend at Tynemouth telling me how you was [sic] behaving yourself. He told me he saw you and a woman from Low Street, half drunk with some Scotch fellows … He heard you saying you were going to the dance. I trusted you dear Moll and I thought you would keep yourself to yourself … If you have got tired of waiting for me or have found anyone else write and tell me so … You had better keep yourself, for I shall come when you little think it.

Other letters followed until, on Saturday 21 July, Emery disappeared from camp. He went to Mary's home address later that day, in full uniform, and again on the Sunday. On one of those occasions he saw Robert Marshall, Mary's father, who 'gave him the advice of a father'. He also saw Mary, and the pair appeared to be on the best of terms. That Saturday evening he turned up at Tynemouth Castle Barracks, now absent without leave from his regiment. He slept at the barracks until about 7.20 on the morning of Monday 23 July, when he disappeared, taking with him a suit of clothes and a cap belonging to Private Peter Flynn. He called at a clothes shop in North Shields, where he sold the shopkeeper, Eileen Anderson, his regimental trousers and bought a jacket. His army tunic was later found abandoned near the barracks.

Emery then went to an ironmonger's in Saville Street, where he saw Thomas Moar and asked if he could sell him a knife. Moar produced several samples, but Emery said none was large enough. Moar produced a large clasp-knife – 'the largest I had' – and Emery asked if he could sharpen it. Moar rubbed it on an oil-stone and Emery paid him a shilling for it.

At about 5 p.m. the same day Emery went to North Shields post office, where he asked Ernest Clark for a telegram. He wrote something in one of the telegram's boxes and Clark, seeing that he wished it to be posted locally, told him the post was just about to be collected and if he, Emery, were to post it now it would be delivered to a North Shields address by six o'clock. (How times have changed.) So Emery bought an envelope and stamp instead and handed the letter to Clark, who noted that it was addressed to Miss M. Marshall, Cross Street, Tynemouth.

The letter was duly delivered to Mary's house. It read, 'Dear Mary, meet me where we were yesterday afternoon, you know where I mean … Do not forget. Meet me as soon as you receive this. S.G. Emery'. Mary's father told her not to go; her decision to ignore his advice would be a fatal one.

Emery had been in the Crescent Tavern about an hour when people began arriving, talking about the murder. He asked someone 'if she was dead', and on being told that she was he said he had seen it happen, adding 'a soldier did it and I'm a soldier myself.' Then he asked the innkeeper, William Robertson, for some writing materials. He was supplied with pen, notepaper and an envelope, and after writing something he put the note into envelope which he gave to Mrs Robertson, writing her name and address on the envelope. He said to her, 'Don't open this until five minutes after I leave.' The conversation and writing the note all took place in the public bar. Mrs Robertson noted that the young man was 'quite sober'.

Not surprisingly, Mrs Robertson became suspicious, but, as it was near closing time and the inn was busy, she did not question him further. Just then her little daughter drew her mother aside and said, 'Don't talk to him, mother, the murderer had a light cap and suit on and he's like him.' After Emery had left, Mrs Robertson opened the envelope. That was just after eleven o'clock. The handwriting was poor, but she was able to discern that Emery had written 'I am the murderer'. She gave the note to her husband who went to the police station and handed it in – just as Emery himself was being brought in, having been arrested by Inspector McKenzie and Sergeant McQueen. Upon seeing Emery, Mrs Robertson declared, 'That's the man who wrote the letter.'

Inspector McKenzie, having seen the lifeless body of Mary Marshall in the church vestry, had made enquiries and had gone looking for Emery. About a quarter to midnight, he and Sergeant McQueen were in Tynemouth Road, conveniently near to the House of Correction, when they saw Emery approaching. He confirmed his name when asked, and produced the knife. As McKenzie made to take it from him Emery lunged at the policeman and attempted to stab him in the stomach. The blade caught his tunic but did not penetrate it. Emery then smiled and said he 'didn't mean it'. On being taken into custody and accused of the murder, Emery said, 'Is she dead?' and on being told she was he said, 'Thank God for that. Can I see her? I would like to see her dead.' He added that, 'I first thought of doing it on the 7th and I thought of it for two days. I came on Saturday for the purpose of doing it.'

★ ★ ★

A few days later, Sergeant McQueen found the telegram and envelope, in pieces, in a ditch, some 1,200 yards away from the murder scene. He was able to paste them together and produced them in evidence.

Superintendent Huish of Tynemouth Borough Police, having attended the scene of the crime, went to the police station where he later took possession from Mary's mother of the letters Emery had sent to Mary from Strenshall Barracks. Emery made a written statement, in which he admitted sending the telegram/letter to Mary, asking her to meet him at Holy Saviour's Church, which she did at 6.10 p.m. on the Monday evening. He said they had walked in the fields until about ten past eight when he 'committed the deed'. He was quite sober, he said. Emery then asked to write to his father, which he did, before tossing it across the desk at Huish, saying, 'You may read it.' Emery had written, simply, 'Dear father, I have murdered Mary'. The police obligingly posted the letter to Emery's father in West Bromwich.

Emery agreed the letters Mary's mother had given to Huish, some 'seven or eight of them', were the ones he had written to Mary. They were couched in 'endearing terms'.

The House of Correction, North Shields. (Author's collection)

He said, 'It was done in this way,' explaining how he murdered Mary after she had put her arms around his neck. To say the evidence against him was overwhelming would be an understatement, and the magistrates had no difficulty in committing him for trial. Yet, although the murder of an innocent young woman had been an horrific and premeditated act, Emery found sympathy and support, and each witness, having testified, was treated to a 'hostile demonstration' and even afterwards followed along Saville Street by several hundred people who 'hooted and yelled' at them, so much so that the police had to send extra officers to ensure order.

Samuel George Emery stood trial at the Northumberland Assizes held at the Moot Hall that November. He pleaded not guilty. Justice Charles presided. Mr Waddy, prosecuting, outlined the facts of the case before calling witnesses, one by one, who provided a chilling sequence of events implicating Emery as Mary's killer. Mr Blake, defending, did not call any witnesses. Indeed, there was no one who could have provided any evidence to support Emery's case.

Summing up, Mr Waddy said that when a person kills another it was for the defence to 'show something which would reduce the crime'. There were only two ways this could be done, he said. One, that the accused was ignorant of the nature and quality of the act he had committed, but the defence had abandoned that. There was no question of Emery's mental condition; he was a man in the prime of health and strength who deliberately and with preparation had killed Mary Marshall. He had been cool, calm and sober. Two, evidence of provocation was something that might justify the act, something to show extenuating circumstances. 'She gave me the chance to do it,' Emery had told the police. That was the moment the poor girl was evidencing her affections for him; that was the moment he chose to strike. 'He slew her practically on the spot.' It was hardly provocation.

The clerk read out Emery's letters, which 'breathed the most passionate affection' for the deceased and were 'of a most impressive character'. In one he wrote, 'I never knew I loved you before. I find I could not do without you. I miss you tonight more than ever'. In another, 'God knows I cannot do without you'. In another he wrote about the deceased's supposed flirtation with the 'Scotch fellows', asking her to 'keep away' and threatening that if she did not keep to herself he would come 'when she little thought of it'.

Mr Blake said he would not say a word against the character of the young woman. He would assume she was 'a good girl'. He told the jury they were not considering a crime by a person who would get reward or advantage from the death of another. 'It was a crime of the heart,' he said, and when they had crimes of that sort they naturally approached them in a more sympathetic spirit. Emery was not a man calculated to commit murder. It was true he bought the knife, but he had no intention to kill Mary when he met her and it was only on a moment of impulse that he perpetrated the deed. On the note Emery posted to Mary on the Monday he argued that there was not sufficient time between writing 'the affectionate epistle' to the deceased to 'the enacting of the unfortunate tragedy' enabling him to plan the murder and kill with malice aforethought. He implored the jury to 'deal mercifully with the unfortunate lad'.

The judge told the jury they 'must not stray from the paths of justice and not allow themselves to be influenced by feelings of pity'. He explained the meaning of malice aforethought, saying that if a person killed another when his own life was not in jeopardy the act was wilful murder. He saw nothing in this case that constituted provocation. The jury took seven minutes to give their verdict. Emery, 'wearing a sickly smile', was returned to the dock to hear it. 'We find him guilty,' the foreman said.

Urging Emery to 'repent the crime', his lordship uttered the dreaded words:

> … that you be taken from hence to the place from whence you came, and from thence to the place of execution and that you be there hanged by the neck until you be dead and that your body be afterwards buried in the precincts in the prison … and may the Lord have mercy on your soul.

After 'looking boldly' around the court Emery smiled and was taken down.

Emery, being 'wonderfully cheerful, with no appearance indicating that he was so near to his end in this world', spent most of the afternoon prior to the day of his execution writing letters – as he had done before and after the commission of his crime – this time to relatives, and comrades in his army regiment. He also wrote to Robert Marshall, asking forgiveness and expressing sorrow for his crime, which, he said, was committed in a temper. A 'numerously signed petition' to have his sentence commuted on the grounds of insanity was rejected by the Home Secretary.

Early on the morning of 11 December 1894 a 'vast concourse of persons' gathered outside Newcastle Prison to witness the hoisting of the black flag that would signal Emery's execution. The *Shields Daily News* wrote poignantly:

> There was a thick haze and a death-like stillness. Now and again the mist lifted and the pale light of the moon caused gruesome shadows to rise up round about the dark sombre gaol. The

street lamps added their feeble glow and intensified the impressive spectacle…There seemed to be death in the air. The terrible spell of anxiety was broken by the Cathedral chimes, followed by the deep solemn tones of the hour-stroke signalling eight o'clock. Hardly had the last note died away before the black flag flew, communicating to those outside the gaol the tidings that all was over.

Unlike in previous years, the press were not permitted to witness the execution. However, it is known that Emery, taken from his cell after 'passing a fairly good night and partaking of a moderately good breakfast', walked firmly to the scaffold and quietly submitted to pinioning by Billington, the executioner. Death was reported as instantaneous.

This was a particularly tragic case, not only for the murder of an innocent young woman, but for the man who murdered her. Samuel George Emery undoubtedly loved or at least had strong feelings for Mary Marshall. He courted her, and, it transpired, even tried to marry her at the register office, despite her father's objection. When he was sent away he wrote to her. His actions, undoubtedly premeditated, were unforgivable: leaving his post, changing his clothes to avoid being recognised, buying a knife which was specially sharpened at his behest, writing a note, enticing her to a spot where he stabbed her repeatedly despite her futile attempts to stop him. Emery said he murdered Mary Marshall in a temper. He was wrong; he murdered her through jealousy.

Today, Mary Marshall's initials are visible at Holy Saviour's churchyard, reputedly inscribed in the stone by the 'young maid' herself. They can be seen atop the wall behind the bus stop on the Broadway.

Carved in stone, Mary Marshall's initials on top of the church wall. (© Paul Heslop, 2011)

Six

'NOT A TITTLE OF EVIDENCE'

Hexham, 1899

George Scholick, aged fifty-three, a widower, lived with his daughter, Hannah, at Mount Pleasant, Hexham. Mr Scholick was employed as a gamekeeper by John Lowes, a wealthy landowner of Wydon Burn. On Tuesday, 6 December, however, Mr Scholick was not gamekeeping. Instead, on 'a wet and miserable day', he left his house at about 8 a.m. and went to Hexham to take chickens to market.

Scholick first walked to Wydon Burn where he collected the poultry, which he placed in a basket. He was then taken into town by John Bowman, Mr Lowes's coachman, who drove him first to Hexham railway station, where Scholick collected more poultry, then to Hexham market place, where Bowman left him. Later, at 11.10 a.m. Bowman's wife, Mary, saw Scholick from their cottage window. He was walking along the reservoir, from the direction of Hexham towards Wydon Burn. He was carrying his basket, which appeared to be empty, and which she would have expected him to leave with Mr Lowes but obviously having passed his house had not done so.

About this time, or slightly earlier, Isaac Reay, a gardener, who was working in a field at Causey Hill nursery, heard gunshots coming from the direction of a plantation known as Benson's Fell Wood, by Yarridge Lane. John Robson, who was working with Reay, also heard the shots. Neither paid much attention, shooting being common practice on John Lowes's land. Soon afterwards, both men saw Scholick, still carrying the basket, hurrying across a field next to the nursery, in the direction of the shots. Ten minutes later more shots were heard. Mrs Bowman, Reay and Robson all knew Scholick by sight; there was no doubt that it was he whom they had seen.

Thomas Suddes, a farmer at Queen's Letch to the east of Benson's Fell Wood, was working outdoors on the nearby Rising Sun Farm among cattle and sheep. For part of the time he was in a field near to Yarridge Lane. Around 11.30 a.m. he popped into the Rising Sun inn opposite the junction with Benson's Fell road end. After only five minutes or so he emerged, and was walking east along the lane when he heard two shots, followed by a third about a minute later. He thought they came from the vicinity of Benson's Fell Wood. He looked but saw no one.

John Maddison, a woodman from Corbridge, was working in another plantation, to the east of Benson's Fell Wood, when sometime between eleven and twelve o'clock he heard shots coming from the direction of the wood. He thought the shots had been fired by a shooting party, although he saw no one. John Bell, a farmer from High Yarridge, was driving along Yarridge Lane about 11.30 towards Benson's Fell Wood, when he heard shots ahead of him. The shots startled his horse. He could see the length of the road ahead, including where it passed the wood, but saw no one. It would not have been difficult for someone to simply conceal himself behind the wall at the field edge, or in the plantation.

The sequence of events appertaining to the shots and the movement of George Sholick, gamekeeper, seem to suggest that as he was walking home he heard shots, and, instead of going home, he hurried towards them. Soon afterwards, more shots were heard by several people, specifically three by Thomas Saddes.

The following day, Wednesday, John Bowman was searching, with others, for the now-missing Mr Scholick. At about 3.30 p.m. he found Scholick's basket lying by a small wicket at the Benson's Fell roadside, near Benson's Fell Farm, just off Yarridge Lane, a location not on Scholick's route home. At 5.45 p.m. the same day, John Moore, of Blackhill Farm, was driving along Yarridge Lane when he stopped his cart at the roadside and went to the wall-side, some fifty yards from the corner of Benson's Fell Wood. Moore never gave explanation for stopping 'in the middle of nowhere', but it may have been to relieve himself, or perhaps he was simply looking around in the knowledge that George Scholick was missing. Moore noticed some branches piled on the ground but ignored them, presuming they had been dumped there by someone driving an overladen cart. He saw them again the next day when he passed, again ignoring them.

There had been much searching of the area on the Wednesday, but no trace was found of George Scholick, although there could have been little doubt that something untoward had happened to him.

The next day, Thursday 8 December, John Maddison was beating for a shooting party. At 12.35 he was on the north side of Yarridge Lane, when he came upon the pile of branches noticed but ignored the previous day by John Moore. Maddison, knowing of the disappearance of George Scholick, lifted one of them and saw a hand. Knowing Scholick was gamekeeper to Mr Lowes, he reported his find to him without delay.

Shortly after one o'clock, the police were on the case when Superintendent Adam Robertson from Hexham went to the scene. Robertson found Scholick's body, still covered with branches, some fifty-three yards from the east corner of Benson's Fell Wood. Dr John Archibald Jackson examined the scene, finding no trace of a struggle, although he noticed what he took to be bloodstains on the other side of Yarridge Lane. The body lay face down, the left arm underneath and the right arm twisted round to the back, palm upward, showing drops of blood. There was a wound on the left temple from which a piece of bone, ¾ inch in size, hung loose. The right coat sleeve was saturated in blood. The body was removed to a nearby farmhouse where Dr Jackson established that George Scholick had died through shotgun wounds.

Yarridge Lane, near Hexham. George Scholick was shot dead just beyond the far end of the wood. (© Paul Heslop, 2011)

The following day, Dr Jackson made a post-mortem examination, finding the left shoulder, upper part of the chest and back riddled with shot. Only a few of the shot had penetrated through clothing to the skin, suggesting a discharge from distance. On the right deltoid muscle – the rounded part of the shoulder – were more shot marks, and evidence of self-defence through the bone of the right arm being shattered, with shot in the bone. Dr Jackson considered these wounds to be caused by a second shot, closer to Mr Scholick, and would have caused him to fall.

The last shot had hit his face; the left ear was split in two and the cheek bone and jaw were fractured. The hair behind the left ear was scorched and the temporal bone was fractured. Pieces of bone were recovered from the brain. This shot had been fired from close range, four feet perhaps, with Mr Scholick lying on the ground, causing instant death. In short, said Dr Jackson, George Scholick had been shot three times: the first in the left shoulder, the second in the right arm, the third into the left temple. He was probably shot on the road and dragged to the place where he was found.

It wasn't long before the police had the name of a suspect. John Lowes, the landowner, had had several complains from his gamekeeper about eighteen-year-old George Dodd, concerning the 'infringement of the sporting rights' on his estate. On the day after the discovery of the body Superintendent Robertson and Inspector Halpin went to Dodd's home address, Benson's Fell, an isolated farm just off Yarridge Lane, ten minutes walk from the scene of the crime.

The policemen, in fact, saw the entire Dodd family: Mr and Mrs Dodd, their two daughters and George. The girls said they had heard shots on the Tuesday, around eleven o'clock, and although they ran outside they had seen no one. George admitted he had left the house about eleven o'clock. When asked for his movements, he said he had walked up the road towards the Rising Sun, then turned right along Yarridge Lane to Yarridge Farm, a route that would have taken him past the spot where George Scholick was murdered. He said he heard the hounds or harriers running to the west, so he ran towards them near Black Hill farm and saw them, but then 'came round' by the steeplechase course to near Plover Hill and down across the fields to the Rising Sun, thence home. No one could verify his movements; he said he heard no shots being fired. He had not taken a gun with him, he added.

Superintendant Robertson asked Dodd's father if he objected to police searching the house. He had no objection and presented the police with a double-barrelled and a single-barrelled shotgun, both muzzle-loading. Inspector Halpin asked George Dodd if he was wearing the same clothes now that he wore on Tuesday. Everything but the coat, Dodd replied. Mrs Halpin fetched her son's coat and the policemen saw a stain on it. Dodd told the policemen, 'I think I can account for the blood [on the coat]. We were killing a pig last week.' Inspector Halpin saw a pig, recently slaughtered, in the outhouse. The policemen were satisfied that the guns were in such condition they could not have been fired recently.

On Sunday evening, 11 December, Inspector Halpin went to Benson's Fell Farm and arrested George Dodd. When charged with murder Dodd protested, 'How can you do that? I am not the man. How can you prove it?'

Dodd appeared before the Hexham magistrates on the Monday. After telling the court of the circumstances of the crime and Dodd's arrest, Superintendent Robertson said that although Dodd had now told him he had seen 'three or four other people' on his walk on the Tuesday, including a man near Black Hill, he had not been able to establish their identities, if they existed, but that he had 'other evidence' he could produce if Dodd was remanded in custody. Dodd was defended by T. W. Welford, who said he had a few questions to ask the superintendent, but Mr Gibson, the clerk, said they would not be hearing evidence that morning. Mr Welford persisted, whereupon the following bizarre exchange took place.

Mr Welford: 'It is such a serious injustice to this young man if you remand him upon a statement the superintendent has made. As far as it goes, there is not a tittle of evidence to incriminate him at the present time. Instead of remanding him, which would attach guilt to him, you can discharge him and he can be brought back the minute you have additional evidence. The law presumes innocence until guilt is proved. There is not a tittle of evidence that he shot this man, nor that the man was shot on the 6th.'

'We are not trying the case,' Mr Gibson, the clerk, said, truthfully.

'I am submitting it to the magistrates,' said Mr Welford. 'I don't see why you should take any such part.' To which the chairman of the bench told him that the clerk was their adviser. 'There is not a tittle of evidence,' Mr Welford repeated. 'We have not gone into the evidence,' said Mr Head, another magistrate. 'Then why remand him?' asked Mr Welford. 'You don't know what evidence we have,' he was told. 'Have you been trying him behind his back?' Mr Welford enquired. 'The superintendent has been sworn and says he has further evidence,' said Mr Gibson. 'There is not a tittle of evidence,' said Mr Welford. Tittle of evidence or not, George Dodd was remanded in custody.

On 15 December, an inquest into the death of George Scholick opened at the Royal Hotel, Hexham. Evidence was taken, of his death and the injuries that caused it, along with what witnesses had to say about events on the Tuesday through to Thursday, when the body was found. The coroner concluded that Mr Scholick had died from three gunshot wounds which could not have been self-inflicted. He adjourned the inquest until 22 December. George Scholick was buried the following day in Greenhead churchyard.

On 19 December, George Dodd again appeared before the Hexham magistrates. Mr W. Pruddah prosecuted; Mr J.E. Joel, a barrister, appeared for Dodd. Not surprisingly, the courtroom was packed. One by one the witnesses testified, as they had done at the inquest. George Scholick had been last seen carrying his basket on Tuesday 6 December; he had been found dead two days later, shot three times, his body hidden beneath a pile of branches. John Lowes, the landowner, confirmed here had been a shooting party out on the Tuesday morning, not on his land but to the west – not in the vicinity of Benson's Fell Wood.

'Death of a Gamekeeper', *Police Illustrated News*. The artist's image bears no resemblance to the actual scene of the crime – nor, indeed, reality. (Author's collection)

Mr Joel asked Lowes if George Scholick, as his gamekeeper of nine years' standing, had had reason to prosecute any poacher. Not within a recent date, replied Mr Lowes. As far as he was aware, Mr Scholick had had no quarrel with any of his tenants. Mr Pruddah asked Lowes if Scholick had ever 'made complaint' to him about anyone. 'I have had complaints, certainly,' said Lowes. When asked to give names, he replied, 'I would rather not.' When Mr Joel objected to this line of questioning, magistrates, after consulting the clerk, instructed Mr Lowes to answer. 'Will you tell us their names?' said Mr Pruddah. 'Principally against George Dodd,' said Lowes, 'three or four times,' he added, adding there were no other names within the past year.

If this was scant evidence that the person who shot George Scholick was George Dodd, the case for the prosecution took a turn for the better when Joseph Nicholson, a farm servant, was called to give evidence. He had worked for John Bell at High Yarridge farm since the Wednesday after the November hirings at Hexham, and the second Sunday afterwards he met George Dodd at the farm. The pair went to High Shield, just down from the Rising Sun, and there met another young man called Telfer Oxley, known as Telf. Dodd and Oxley, who were already acquainted, went into the barn, leaving Nicholson at the gate. Then they went into the stable and invited Nicholson to join them inside. Nicholson said that Dodd told him the shooters would be out on the Monday, adding 'we will have a day too.'

Oxley showed Dodd a breech-loading gun and cartridge, saying it was handy if he, Nicholson, ever 'wanted it a day'. It was kept in a corner of the stable, in a bin. Dodd told Oxley to tell his brother to 'fetch him a shilling box of shot from Phipps's'. On the way home, Dodd told Nicholson the gamekeeper was 'dead nuts' on him (Dodd) and Oxley. Nicholson said he saw Dodd one Tuesday morning, although he couldn't remember which, when Dodd had been carrying a gun in a bag. 'It's my gun,' Dodd told him. He also saw Dodd on the Wednesday before the body was found, when Dodd has asked him pointedly if he had seen the hounds on the Tuesday. He saw him again at 7.40 p.m. on the Thursday, when Dodd asked him if he had seen any 'poacher-like fellow' in the fields or if he had heard any shots. Nicholson said no to both questions.

The prosecution would have hoped that the testimony of Dr Murray, who examined the dark red stain on the right sleeve, would be helpful. Bloodstains would have considerably supported the case against George Dodd. Bloodstains they were: Dr Murray said he had examined the coat by inserting a few pieces of the material in a saline solution, then examined the fluid from it under a microscope. It was mammalian blood, said Dr Murray, adding that he could not say it was human. The moment he uttered these words, a round of applause went through the courtroom. In those days, blood grouping, or even identifying whether blood was from a human or animal, was not possible.

There was evidence about the harriers that had been out on the day of the murder. A hunt in progress meant people crossing the fields, but the harriers were not in the vicinity of the murder, although anyone associated with the hunt may have been. But no one was seen, other than those George Dodd said he had seen that day, all of which was uncorroborated. As to the testimony of Superintendent Robertson, who had endeavoured to build a conclusive case against Dodd, one question by Mr Joel undermined the case, to say the least; Mr Joel asked, 'Has a living soul told you they saw George Dodd about the lane?' Superintendant Robertson: 'No.' Mr Joel said he had had no more reason to go to Mr Dodd's farm than, say, Mr Oxley's. In fact, Superintendant Robertson did go to Oxley's, but was satisfied that Telford Oxley was at Hexham Market at the time of the murder. One hopes he also established satisfactorily that Joseph Nicholson was elsewhere too. Telford Oxley showed Superintendant Robertson his gun, which the superintendent thought had been recently used. But if it had been, in those days, in the fields of rural England, that would hardly have been unusual.

Mr Joel was left with the simple task of telling the court that there was no evidence to justify remanding George Dodd in custody again, and urged the bench to dismiss the case. After retiring for a few minutes the magistrates said they could not justify sending Dodd for trial, and, to loud and prolonged cheering, he was discharged. As Dodd left the building, the *Hexham Courant* reported, 'a scene of wild enthusiasm and cheering followed the decision of the bench, whilst huge crowds blocked the exits of the court to catch a glimpse of the released man who seemed to have the good wishes of all'. The prosecution simply did not have enough evidence to convince the magistrates to send Dodd for trial. Not a tittle, in fact.

Seven

'STRAWS OF EVIDENCE'

Cullercoats, 1901

John Miller (senior) was a hawker and had lived with his wife, Mary, at 19 Dove Street, Cullercoats. Mr Miller had worked hard and when he died he left all his money to his widow. The house was made up into two flats, with Mary living upstairs and two lodgers, Joseph Ferguson and his son, in the other. The Millers had had three sons, all who lived locally and were not best pleased when their mother married the lodger, Joseph Ferguson. At some point Ferguson's son moved away, and in 1900 Mr and Mrs Ferguson, as Mary now was, moved to an upstairs flat at 55 Hudlestone Street, Cullercoats.

At that time Mary was about eighty-five years of age; her new husband was sixty, younger than at least one of Mary's sons, sixty-seven-year-old John Miller. The reason for Mary's family's chagrin was that Joseph Ferguson, and not they, stood to inherit Mary's money and her property when she died. Nevertheless, Mary would say that there had been no quarrels since her marriage, and she had helped different members of her family out from time to time. As for Joseph Ferguson, he was a quiet, peaceful man; a joiner by trade, he was now retired and able to rely on his wife's money to pay the bills.

Although sixty-seven, John Miller, Mary's son, could not retire, and had to earn a living through running 'amusements' on Tynemouth Long Sands. He had good cause, in his opinion at least, to resent the privileged life Joseph Ferguson had. John Miller had a nephew, thirty-year-old John Robert Miller. John Robert was a sort of busker, who played the harp in various towns throughout the north. On Friday, 20 September 1901, John Robert Miller had intended to travel to Brampton, in Cumberland, but missed the train. So he wandered into North Shields where he met up with his uncle, and the pair went drinking.

At about 2.30 p.m. that day the Millers went to Henry Purvis's ironmonger's shop in Saville Street, North Shields. Purvis recognised John Miller, whom he had known for

Tynemouth Long Sands, where John Miller ran his 'amusements'. (Reproduced by kind permission of Andrew Clark and George Nairn)

twenty years; the younger man he had never seen before, although he would later describe him as 'rather dazed'. 'We want to look at some knives,' said John Miller. Purvis placed eighteen knives on the counter for their perusal. After both Millers examined the knives, John Miller said, 'These are not the kind of knives we want,' and indicating his nephew added, 'he is going to sea in a ship as a cook.' 'It's a sheath knife you want,' said Purvis, and showed one to them, but John Miller said it was too big.

Purvis then produced a number of knives with shorter blades. John Miller selected one and said, 'This knife will do.' 'You will want a sheath and belt,' said Purvis, who produced a sheath and went to get some belts. John Robert Miller slotted the knife into the sheath, which Purvis took from him and fitted to a belt. But John Robert handed the belt back to Purvis, saying he would take only the knife and sheath. John Robert paid for his purchase, but, as they were leaving the shop, Purvis noticed him handing some coppers to John Miller.

The Millers were next seen in Cullercoats, sometime after three o'clock, by Zephaniah Miller (no relation), a cab proprietor, who saw the pair leaning over some railings, looking out to sea, and soon afterwards enter the Bay Hotel and come out again only a minute or so later. They walked off in the direction of Dove Street back lane, then towards Hudlestone Street. Zephaniah Miller took particular notice of them because they were 'very drunk', the younger man particularly.

Shortly afterwards, when Mary Ferguson heard a knock at the front door, her husband rose to go downstairs to answer. She tried to prevent him from doing so, saying she would answer herself. He went downstairs nonetheless. At that time Robert Stephenson Oliver, thirteen, a message boy, happened to be leaving Robinson's shop, which was situated almost opposite the Fergusons' house. Master Oliver saw the two Millers at the Fergusons' door, and the younger man knock 'twice or thrice', whilst the older Miller stepped into a nearby doorway as though to conceal himself. Oliver saw the door of number 55 opened by someone on the inside, although he could not say by whom. John Robert Miller entered at once, to be followed by John Miller, upon which the door was closed.

Events were also witnessed by James Melville from his grocer's shop, on the opposite side of the street. He too saw John Robert Miller knock at the door as John Miller concealed himself; he too saw the door being opened, and he identified the person opening it as Joseph Ferguson. He saw John Robert rush in, followed by John Miller, 'hot on his heels'. The door was closed, and a short time later Melville heard a dog bark from inside the house.

Inside, from the top of the stairs, Mary Ferguson saw her husband open the door and two men enter. They did not speak, but she saw one of them attack her husband with a knife, although she could not – or would not – say which one. Since she saw the attack, we can assume she recognised the men, who were her son and grandson respectively. James Melville then saw Mary appear at an upstairs window calling out that her husband had been stabbed.

Joseph Ferguson had been stabbed to death at the bottom of the darkened stairway of his home. After the deed, one of the men ran upstairs and said to Mary, 'Do you see this knife?' 'Yes, you villain,' she replied, 'you have killed my husband.' 'Yes I have,' the man said. The other man then came upstairs too. Mary Ferguson would never say which of the two had the knife. John Miller and John Robert Miller then left the house by the back door.

They didn't get far. Several neighbours had responded to Mary Ferguson's cries and ran along the lane at the back of the house. One of them was Zephaniah Miller, the cab proprietor. On being told that Joseph Ferguson had been stabbed he ran up the back lane and into the back of the house. When Mary saw him she said, simply, 'They have killed Mr Ferguson.' She handed him a candle and he went into the passage where he saw the body of Joseph Ferguson lying at the foot of the stairs. His face was covered in blood and there were marks as though he had been stabbed in the neck. Zephaniah Miller then went to the back of the house where he saw John and John Robert Miller, and told the crowd to 'take hold' of them.

Isabella Mason, who lived close by, saw John Miller and John Robert Miller and Mrs Ferguson standing in the lane. Mrs Ferguson told her, 'They have stabbed Ferguson.' Mrs Mason saw John Robert Miller washing his hands in the yard. Seeing her, he said, 'Feel my head,' which he then commenced to wash in a tub of water. Then she heard John Robert say to John Miller, 'You tantalised me. You irritated me. You gave me the drink. You gave me the knife.' As the Millers were forced to wait by the crowd, John Miller calmly set about lighting his pipe, even enquiring if anyone had a match.

When Constable Matthew Whitehead arrived, he was directed to the place where Joseph Ferguson's body lay, and, on making his way to the back of the house, he found the bloodstained knife at the foot of the stairs. He then arrested John and John Robert Miller, who were taken to North Shields police station. Doctors Phillips and Brumwell attended the scene, in company with Inspector Henry McQueen. The doctors declared then and there that Joseph Ferguson's death was 'due to haemorrhage due to the severance of the carotid artery'.

Later, Dr Brumwell examined John Robert Miller in the police station. Miller said to him, 'I done it doctor. Take and hang me. I have murdered my uncle.' John Miller was about to say something when Sergeant Proud cautioned them both against saying anything. Notwithstanding this, John Robert Miller said, 'It's all right. I am going to die. I've done something to make me die. It's true I've committed murder. I will die a coward. Never before God had I any intention of doing it. I will go to the scaffold and die. I feel miserable to think I had no provocation to do it.' John Robert's face and hands were stained with blood, as were his clothes. He was very drunk. John Miller said, 'I tied to prevent the affair but I could not. I have as little to do with it as you have.'

The following Monday, at North Shields police station, Dr Brumwell examined John Robert Miller again. The doctor asked him if he knew where he was. 'In a tram car,' Miller told him.

'In what town?' asked the doctor.

'Sunderland,' replied Miller.

How had he hurt his hand?

'When I did the murder.'

Why did he do it?

'Because we had some words.' said Miller.

Dr Brumwell thought John Robert Miller was 'on the border of *delirium tremens* (delirious disorder of the brain through alcohol) or alcoholic insanity. When, subsequently, both men appeared at the magistrates' court, Mary Ferguson, when asked by John Miller to confirm that her late husband had 'often given him a shilling', she concurred, and agreed that she could not think of an occasion when they had quarrelled. When they were

Cullercoats, the Bay Hotel is on the left. It has since been demolished. (Reproduced by kind permission of Andrew Clark and George Nairn)

formally charged before the magistrates with murdering Joseph Ferguson, John Miller replied, 'I am not guilty in word or deed.' John Robert Miller said nothing.

John Miller and his nephew, John Robert Miller, stood trial at the Moot Hall, Newcastle, in November, before Justice Grantham. Mr J.E. Joel called witnesses to prove the prosecution's case, that both men were guilty, notwithstanding it could not be positively established who actually stabbed Joseph Ferguson to death, even though John Robert Miller had several times stated unequivocally that is was he. The case was based on 'joint enterprise', that both men had sought the death of Mr Ferguson.

When eighty-five-year-old Mary Ferguson stepped into the witness box, she did so with 'something bulky' underneath her coat. It turned out to be a puppy. The poor woman was allowed to keep it when testifying. How difficult it must have been for her; widowed through the murder of her husband, yet having to testify against her own son and grandson, both of whom faced death if convicted. Who could blame her for stating, on one hand, that there had never been any quarrel between her late husband and the men in the dock, whilst, on the other, she had to say that it was they who had come to her house and had committed the crime.

She did, however, throw some light on the previous history of John Robert Miller, saying that when he was a boy he had been kicked on the head by a horse, at least that's what his mother had told her; and further, she had heard he had been struck by a cock-shy (something thrown, as in a coconut shy). 'But it did not kill him,' she added, to laughter in court. She knew John Miller was sightless in one eye. 'It would be better if had lost the other eye,' she said to more laughter, a statement that betrayed her feelings perhaps.

Defending, Horace Marshall told the court he intended to prove John Robert Miller 'was in a mental condition that did not make him responsible for his actions'. Dr Hingston, medical superintendent of the Yorkshire North Riding Asylum, confirmed that John Robert was in the asylum from November 1898 until February 1899, suffering from mania, which resulted from drink. He too said John Robert had been kicked in the head by a horse, an injury that had made him more liable to attacks of insanity than an 'ordinary man'. He suffered from *delirium tremens*. When asked if this was caused by drinking alcohol, he replied, 'It's leaving off the drink suddenly that causes it.' Dr Hingston said that when John Robert left the asylum he had cautioned him, considering he would be 'very easily led'. 'If he had kept from drink he would have been all right,' said the doctor. 'Would he know the difference between right and wrong?' his lordship enquired. 'I could not say,' was the best the good doctor could offer.

Dr Callcott, medical superintendent at Coxlodge Asylum, said John Robert Miller had told him he remembered being in Cullercoats on 20 September, the day of the crime, and after missing his train he went to North Shields to see his uncle. He said he would sometimes drink as much as two bottles of whisky in one day and frequently suffered from attacks of *delirium tremens*. John Robert did not recall going to the ironmonger's to buy a knife, said Dr Callcott. He said if his brain had been injured (when kicked in the head by a horse) he would be more liable to be affected by drink; but then, if he could play the harp, he must know what he was doing. Dr Hardcastle of Newcastle Gaol told the court that John Robert was 'free from delusions and insanity', and since being in custody he had 'improved in health and mind'. What the jury made of these combined testimonies one can only wonder.

Mr Marshall, called John Robert Miller's brother, James, a harpmaker, who said he recalled John Robert being kicked the head by a horse when he was about seven years of age, after which he had become a 'semi-maniac'. James Miller had kept birds; there had been an occasion when John Robert had opened the cage door and allowed them to escape. On another occasion John Robert had struck him in the face with a glass for no reason, and had then ran outside and bit himself on the arm. Mr Joel asked James Miller whether he thought that when John Robert gave his birds their 'natural freedom' it was out of humanity, but James thought he was mad. John Robert's mother said he had been kicked in the head by a horse when he was seven. 'From being a sharp, intelligent lad, he became a dull idiot. He was called "Silly Jack", he was so stupid.'

Addressing the jury on behalf of John Robert Miller, Horace Marshall suggested he had no motive for killing Joseph Ferguson, nor had there been any gain. On the day of the crime John Robert had missed his train and started to drink heavily. When the pair had gone to Purvis's shop to buy the knife, John Robert had played no part in its purchase. It was John Miller, he said, who did the talking. His uncle was the 'real purchaser', and when there was change John Robert handed it to him. And even if Ferguson had been stabbed by John Robert, was he responsible? His brain had been affected by being kicked by a horse when he was a boy. In the workhouse in Yorkshire he was suffering not from *delirium tremens* but strange delusions, believing he was going to be killed by an 'infernal machine'. He saw coffins filled with men armed with knives. Marshall suggested that on the day of the crime John Robert Miller was 'in that mood'. The old man (Joseph Ferguson) had been angry and might have provoked those delusions. John Robert was not morally or legally responsible for his actions. It was different from the case where two men were concerned in a murder and their minds were turned in the same direction.

Mitchell-Innes, for John Miller, said he was conscious of an 'undercurrent' of sympathy for John Robert Miller, on account of his youth and weakness of mind. But he asked the jury

Front Street, Cullercoats. These houses have long since been demolished. (Reproduced by kind permission of Andrew Clark and George Nairn)

to consider the facts. No one, he said, would contend that it was John Miller who struck the fatal blow. There had been three or four confessions by John Robert Miller. John Miller was only in court because of a technical rule, that if one man consorted with another to commit murder he too was guilty. Didn't the ferocity of the attack show that John Robert was a maniac? He suggested that John Miller waited outside the Fergusons' flat until John Robert got whatever he went in for and that when heard the disturbance he rushed in after him. 'These straws of evidence were too weak to bear the theories of the prosecution.'

The judge told the jury they had to decide whether one or both prisoners were guilty. If the condition of the mind of John Robert Miller meant he could not suffer penalty – meaning he may have been insane – that did not prevent the older man from being liable if he had made a tool of the younger man. It seemed to him that John Miller knew what was being done, and that he induced John Robert to take the life of James Ferguson. John Robert's mind was not 'well balanced', but he had given way to drinking, and there was no doubt he was drunk.

He closed by saying that if two people were together for a common object each was liable for the act of the other. The jury took just twelve minutes to agree that both men were guilty of murder. Asked what they had to say, John Miller replied, 'I am perfectly agreeable to the sentence of death. But I may assure you on the word of a man that I am not afraid to meet my Maker. I am innocent.' John Robert Miller said, 'I have nothing to say, only that I did not know what I was doing or I should not have done it. God bless everybody.'

His lordship told John Robert Miller, 'No doubt you have been accustomed to drinking heavily and you previously suffered, as a result of your drinking, *delirium tremens*. But there has been no evidence produced that would justify saying you were not responsible for your actions.' To John Miller he said, 'You went with the younger man, he was under your influence and although he was much the worse for drink and was responsible for his actions you could have controlled him if you had tried. You were there with him. You were standing close to him. You could have prevented it. You did not do so and it is impossible to come to any other conclusion that you knew what was going to happen.'

Both Millers were sentenced to hang in Newcastle Prison on 7 December. The hangmen would be William Billington and John Ellis. It had been the authorities' intention to hang both together, but there were hints of trouble for John Robert Miller saw himself as a victim of his uncle's plot. Instead, they decided to hang John Robert at 8 a.m., his uncle at 9.30. For Ellis, the executions, his first, would turn out to be a traumatic experience, for through the night, as he lay in his bed, he heard the constant screams of John Robert Miller who was facing his impending death with dread. However, when the two hangmen entered John Robert's cell, they found him quiet, 'looking with a dull moroseness'.

As they led him to the scaffold, John Robert saw the prison governor, the chaplain and other officials. 'What are all these people here for?' he enquired, before calmly turning and walking away – only to be turned about and led to the trapdoor. His executioners worked quickly, strapping his feet, and slipping the noose over his head, then the white cap. When Billington pulled the lever he died instantly. An hour and a half later, John Miller went to his death calmly. The customary black flag was raised above the prison wall, signalling the fate of the two condemned men.

Eight

A LUST FOR GOLD

Alnmouth, 1910

Thomas Charlton was foreman porter at Alnmouth railway station. His duties included checking trains at journey's end, a task he undertook on the recently-arrived 12.06 p.m. train from Newcastle. It was Friday 18 March, just another routine day.

Having regard to events that day, it is important to know details of the train, specifically the carriages and their compartments.

The train comprised a locomotive that pulled four carriages, each of three compartments. Each compartment had two rows of seats, one where passengers sat with their backs to the engine, and one opposite, where passengers faced forward. Unlike today, there was no communication between carriages and compartments.

Charlton checked the empty train by starting at the fourth carriage, the one at the rear. He then checked the third carriage, then the second. When he came to the first carriage, the one next to the engine, he opened the door of the rear compartment. As soon as he did so he saw blood on the floor. It seemed to emanate from underneath the seat facing the engine. What his feelings would have been as he stepped inside, one can barely imagine; but there, on the floor under the seat, lay the body of a man. He was lying face down; close by were his hat and broken spectacles, and a return ticket from Widdrington to Newcastle. There were also some mysterious wisps of paper, although it is doubtful if Charlton noticed these. Charlton reported his find and the police attended.

The man was John Innes Nisbet, aged forty-four, of Heaton Road, Newcastle, a bookkeeper employed by Rayne and Burn of Sandhill, Newcastle. Nisbet had worked for the company for twenty-eight years. Like Thomas Charlton, Nisbet's job that day was routine, namely that on alternative Fridays he was issued with a cheque to cover payment of miners' wages at Stobswood Colliery, near Widdrington, on this

Murder victim: John Nisbet.
(Author's collection)

occasion £370 9s 6d, which he presented at Lloyds Bank, Collingwood Street, Newcastle, receiving 231 gold sovereigns, 206 gold half sovereigns, £35 0s 9s in silver and £1 0s 6d in copper. Nisbet put it all into a large leather bag, which he locked. The bag weighed one and a half stones (9.5 kg), a heavy and conspicuous item to carry.

As always, Nisbet went to Newcastle Central station where he bought a return ticket to Widdrington. As always, he took the 10.27 Alnmouth train. Only on this occasion he didn't get off at Widdrington; he never got off the train at all, for at some point on the journey he was murdered. When it was discovered that the bag with its valuable contents was missing it was apparent that this was a premeditated crime, and that the motive was robbery. The post-mortem examination revealed that Nisbet had been shot five times in the head. Four of the bullets were recovered and found to be of different calibres: two were of .250 calibre and nickel-coated; two were .320 calibre and made of lead. This suggested two guns had been used, which in turn suggested that maybe two people had shot Nisbet, or that his assailant had discharged two guns.

★ ★ ★

In 1910 there were fourteen stations between Newcastle and Alnmouth. It was normal for Nisbet to speak to his wife, Cicely, from within the last carriage when the train stopped at the first station, Heaton. On this day things were different, for whereas Mrs Nisbet was waiting at the end of the platform where the rear of the train would be, today she spotted her husband leaning out of the window of the first carriage and had to run along the platform to speak to him. 'You won't be later than six o'clock, mind,' Mrs Nisbet told him. 'Auntie is coming.' 'I will come straight home after I've been to the office,' he replied.

As they spoke, Cicely Nisbet noticed a man seated in the same compartment as her husband. The man had his collar turned up and his hat pulled down. The shadow of the tunnel entrance prevented her from getting a clear view of him. However, she would later say she was certain there was no other person in that compartment.

On 21 March, three days after the murder, the *Newcastle Daily Journal* reported that Nisbet's employers were offering a reward of £100 for information leading to the discovery and conviction of the murderers, bizarrely adding, *not being the actual murderer*, as though he or they would step forward. Thanks to fellow-travellers on the train coming forward, the paper was able to give the description of a suspect: '35-40 years, 5 ft 6 in tall, medium build, dark moustache, wearing a light overcoat, black felt hat and appearing well-to-do'. Today, the 'dark moustache' – wide and tapering

A plan showing the route of the 10.27 a.m. Newcastle to Alnmouth train. (© Paul Heslop, 2011)

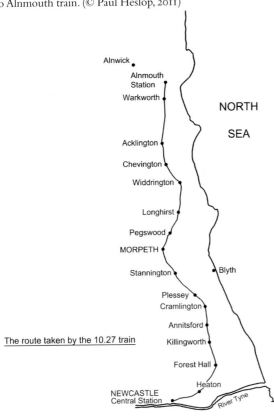

to a point — would make anyone conspicuous, but in 1910 such moustaches were commonplace.

The first two witnesses to come forward were Percival Harding Hall and John William Spink, employees of the Netherton Coal Company, who, like Nisbet, were carrying miners' wages and who had taken the same train. They had travelled on the same train as Nisbet for years and had spoken casually from time to time. Hall and Spink were seated in the middle compartment of the first carriage when, looking through the window, they saw Nisbet, accompanied by a man they did not recognise, walking towards their carriage. They got into the compartment immediately behind the one Hall and Spink occupied.

Hall and Spink got off the train at Stannington. There being no footbridge, they were obliged to wait until the train departed before they could cross the tracks. When waiting, they saw Nisbet still sitting in the last compartment of the first carriage, facing the engine. Nisbet must have seen Hall too, for the two nodded in mutual acknowledgement. Hall noticed another person in the compartment, seated with his back to the engine. Of significance was that Nisbet was alive at Stannington when the train pulled away.

Another traveller on the 10.27 that morning was Wilson Hepple, an artist. Hepple had known a man called John Dickman for twenty years. He first saw him that morning as he waited to buy his ticket, then again a few minutes later on platform 5 when he, Hepple, lingered on the platform before stepping into the third carriage, when he saw Dickman approaching with a man he did not know. The pair went to the first carriage, where the man held the door open for Dickman and both men entered.

Hepple, naturally, mentioned Dickman's name to the police, as being someone he had seen that Friday morning. So, around five o'clock on Monday 21 March, three days after the crime, Dickman, who lived at Jesmond, found himself opening his door to Detective Inspector Andrew Tait, who said he had information that he, Dickman, had been seen on the station platform at Newcastle on Friday morning and could he help the police in any way. It seems that at the time the police considered Dickman to be a witness, nothing more.

Dickman told Tait he had known Nisbet for years, and that he had seen him in the station that Friday morning. 'We must have travelled by the same train,' he said, adding, 'I would have told the police if I thought it would do any good.' Tait asked him – still treating him as a witness, presumably – if he 'would mind' accompanying him to the police station to make a statement. Dickson readily agreed. Tait assured his wife he would be home for tea. In fact, John Dickman never came home again.

At the police station Dickman made a statement, in which he said that he had gone to Newcastle Central station on the Friday morning, where he purchased a return ticket to Stannington. He saw Nisbet in the ticket office; Nisbet said 'Good morning' to him. He, Dickman, then bought a newspaper, the *Manchester Sporting Chronicle*, which was of particular interest as it was Grand National Day. He then went to the refreshment room where he had a pie and a glass of ale before proceeding to the platform, where he took a seat 'nearer the hinder end of the train than the front end'. Not the first carriage, then.

The train, he said, passed Stannington without him noticing – he was engrossed in his newspaper – so he alighted at Morpeth where he handed his ticket to the ticket collector, paying the excess fare of twopence-halfpenny. Dickman then gave the following account of his movements.

The purpose of his journey that day was to visit William Hogg, a colliery contractor at the Dovecote Colliery, near Stannington, regarding new sinkings at the mine, then to call at the Lansdale Drift nearby. He took the 10.27 train from Newcastle Central. He was not alone in his chosen compartment on the train, but he was so engrossed in his newspaper he could not recall any of the other passengers, and had even failed to notice his arrival at Stannington. Having paid the excess fare at Morpeth, Dickman decided to walk first to the Lansdale Drift, then go to Dovecote Colliery.

Dickman said he left Morpeth on the main Newcastle Road, but after walking for half an hour he had taken ill with a serious bout of diarrhoea, so had gone into a field to relieve himself. He also suffered from piles, which were causing him much pain, so he lay on the ground until he felt well enough to continue on his way, by which time he had changed his mind about his intended visits and walked back to Morpeth. He missed the express to Newcastle and so, with half an hour to spare, he wandered into the town where, perchance, he bumped into an acquaintance, Edwin Elliott, who was with another man whom he did not know but who turned out to be William Sanderson.

The three men chatted, mainly about the Grand National, before he, Dickman, returned to the station where he caught the 1.40 train to Newcastle. Before we move on, however, we should note that at Morpeth railway station a man named John Grant happened to board the train Dickman said he had left. Grant walked past the rear compartment of the first carriage – the one John Nisbet occupied – and noticed it was empty before getting into the first compartment of that carriage. If this was so, we may assume Nisbet was already lying dead on the floor and that his killer had probably left the train at Morpeth.

On the day of his arrest Dickman was charged with the murder of John Nisbet. There was evidence to suggest he was Nisbet's killer: he failed to come forward after hearing about the murder, despite the fact that by his own account he knew the victim and saw him at the station; and the sum of £17 9s 5d was recovered from his person, of which £17 was wrapped inside a Lloyds Bank bag, similar to the ones issued to Nisbet on the fateful day. Significantly, his assertion that he occupied a rear carriage was in conflict with Hepple's account, that he knew Dickman and had seen him enter the *first* carriage. Police searched Dickman's home but found no trace of firearms or ammunition or stolen gold and silver. To the charge Dickman replied, 'It is absurd for me to deny the charge because it is absurd to make it. I absolutely deny it.'

A few days later the police held an identification parade to see if the two witnesses, Hall and Spink, could pick Dickman out. Spink failed to identify him. Hall, having walked along the line of nine men, approached a police officer and enquired what he should do. 'Point him out,' said the policeman. Hall then turned to the line and picked out Dickman. He told police, 'I won't swear that the man I pointed out was the man I saw get in [the train] with Mr Nisbet, but if I could be assured that the murderer was there I would have no hesitation in pointing the prisoner out.' An identification of

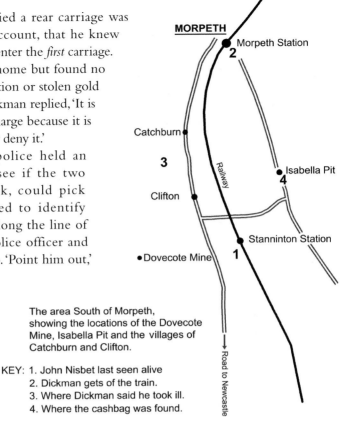

The area South of Morpeth, showing the locations of the Dovecote Mine, Isabella Pit and the villages of Catchburn and Clifton.

KEY: 1. John Nisbet last seen alive
2. Dickman gets of the train.
3. Where Dickman said he took ill.
4. Where the cashbag was found.

A plan showing the area south of Morpeth.
(© Paul Heslop, 2011)

sorts, then; but as things would transpire, the entire identification process was so worthless it ought not to have had any bearing on the case, although, sadly for John Dickman, the malpractice by the police, as it was, wasn't revealed until after his trial although it did come to light before his appeal.

The case was first heard before the magistrates, when Cicely Nisbet gave evidence of the brief encounter with her husband at Heaton station. Until that time she had not been able to provide police with any useful information about the man she said she saw in the same compartment as her husband. But now, as she was leaving the witness box, and seeing Dickman in the dock, she said she recognised him as the same man she had seen on the train, which caused her to faint in the courtroom.

Dickman was committed for trial, but before then there was a significant development in the case. On 9 June Peter Spooner, a colliery manager, found the stolen leather bag during a routine inspection at the bottom of an airshaft at the Isabella Pit, south of Morpeth. The bag had been cut open and most of its contents stolen; only some payslips and a few coins remained. There was no sign of the gold and silver. Whatever fingerprint techniques were in place at time, none was ever found to connect Dickman with the bag, or the scene of the crime for that matter.

Before examining events that unfolded at Dickman's trial, it is worth briefly looking at his antecedents and habits. Dickman spent his formative years living with his parents at Whickham. That was when he and Wilson Hepple became acquainted. Dickman married in 1892, and by 1901 he and his wife were living in Rothbury Terrace, Heaton. After losing his job due to a slump he found work as a secretary at a colliery at Morpeth, when he became much-travelled on the Newcastle to Morpeth train.

At the time of John Nisbet's murder John and Annie Dickman were living at 1 Lily Avenue, Jesmond. By that time it is fair to say that, whatever else he was, John Dickman was a professional gambler with a penchant for horseracing, through which he was closely associated with one Frank Christie. Dickman was also a bookmaker, which was then an offence, so he required a secretive forwarding address; he had one, at a newsagents at Groat Street, Newcastle.

Dickman had financial worries. In October 1909 he borrowed £20 from a Newcastle moneylender, paying only the interest and then introducing to the moneylender Frank Christie, who borrowed £200. At his trial the prosecution would seek to show that he was trying to earn commission by introducing Christie, as well as being unable to pay off his own loan. Thus, it was inferred, John Dickman was broke and this was the reason he robbed John Nisbet and murdered him.

John Alexander Dickman stood trial at the Moot Hall in July before Lord Coleridge. Mr Tindal Atkinson prosecuted; Mr Mitchell-Innes defended. Public entry was by ticket only, such was the clamour for places. The prosecution sought to show that John Nisbet, having boarded the 10.27 train at Newcastle, had been seen alive on the train at Stannington station, but at Morpeth John Grant, who had looked into the compartment occupied by Nisbet, had seen no one; it was assumed therefore that Nisbet was dead by the time the train reached Morpeth, and that he had been shot by John Dickman.

Wilson Hepple was the only person who could positively say he saw Dickman on the station platform at Newcastle, and that he had had been in company with another man with whom he boarded the train. But Hepple did not know Nisbet so his testimony fell short of positively placing Dickman and Nisbet together. Hall and Spink knew Nisbet, but not the man he was with. This led to the sorry tale of the identification parade.

Facing the line-up of nine men, Hall selected Dickman as the man he had seen with Nisbet, but only with the proviso that 'if I could be assured the murderer was there'. What sort of identification was that? Either he recognised Dickman as the man or he did not. Mitchell-Innes suspected there something wrong with the identification procedure; unfortunately, that 'something wrong' was not revealed until after Dickman had been convicted. As it was, the jury were told that a witness had identified Dickman as the man seen with John Nisbet. Mrs Nisbet's 'identification', that the man she saw in the dock at the magistrates' court was the man she saw in the train, was given short shrift.

Dickman, by his own account, got off the train at Morpeth and set off, on foot, to visit Dovecote Colliery, becoming ill on the way and so turning back. Neither the ticket collector, to whom he paid the excess fare, nor the two men he encountered at Morpeth, Edwin Elliott and William Sanderson, noticed him carrying a heavy bag.

Much was made of Dickman's lifestyle, his debts and the implication that there was every reason he would rob and murder Nisbet. This led to the testimony of Henrietta Hymen.

Lord Coleridge, the trial judge in the Dickman case. (Author's collection)

Ms Hymen was the manageress of the newsagents in Groat Street, Newcastle, used by Dickman in his capacity as a bookmaker in the name of F. Black. Ms Hymen knew letters sent to the shop for Dickman were in connection with betting. Sometimes there were parcels, she said, adding 'one parcel contained a gun'. This had not been collected and after a few weeks a postcard had arrived from a company in Glasgow asking for the return of the gun, which had been 'sent in error'. Mr Black [Dickman] had collected the gun, asking for a label so he could return it. There had been an earlier parcel too, wrapped in brown paper and string. She thought it was shaped like a gun and Mr Black had collected it. Amazingly, Dickman was never questioned on the latter parcel. It should be said that at that time there was nothing unusual in owning and buying guns and ammunition. Even so, the implications of Ms Hymen's testimony are obvious, even though no gun was found in Dickman's house.

Andrew Kirkwood, who worked for Pape's gunsmiths, Newcastle, produced a register in which there was an entry showing that an automatic magazine pistol had been sold to 'John A. Dickman, Lily Avenue, Jesmond'. Unfortunately the person who actually sold the gun was not the person giving evidence, so Kirkwood's testimony was inadmissible. One wonders why such a crucial point was simply shrugged off by the court. Did Dickman buy the gun or not? We do not know.

With regard to the two sizes of bullets used to shoot Nisbet, .250 and .320, it seems there was conflicting evidence about whether they could both have been discharged by the same weapon. The wisps of paper found on the floor of the compartment where Nisbet had been shot suggested they had been used as packing for some of the bullets, to make their discharge possible. Yet evidence was given by an 'expert', whose opinion was that two guns must have been used. Another crucial point, again not satisfactorily answered. Perhaps it couldn't be.

Dickman opted to testify. Whatever he had to say, his life depended on it, even though the evidence against him was circumstantial and generally inconclusive. Of Hall's identification, Dickman said he felt Hall had been 'pushed forward' by the police; the gun sent to the newsagent's he said he had returned to sender; the bank bag found in his possession he had had for ten years; marks on his clothing ('blood', said the prosecution; 'bicycle oil', said Dickman) provided answers about his financial troubles, true or untrue, no one could possibly know. Prosecuting counsel asked him to explain in detail the 'infirmities' that obliged him to return to Morpeth, although the specifics on haemorrhoids were thankfully omitted.

Lord Coleridge, said that if Dickman was Nisbet's travelling companion that day there could be 'no reasonable doubt he was the killer'. That's what the prosecution had to prove: that the case against Dickman was proved beyond reasonable doubt. After three and a half hours the jury returned, but before asking them their verdict the judge was obliged to refer to a serious mistake on behalf of prosecuting counsel, Tindal Atkinson.

Summing up after hearing the evidence, Tindal Atkinson had commented about Dickman's wife not being called to give evidence. This may not seem important, but the law had been changed to allow the spouse of an accused to appear in their defence if they so chose, *but if a spouse elected not to appear, the prosecution was not permitted to mention this to the jury*. Tindal Atkinson had done just that, 'inadvertently' he would say, although once said, the jury had heard it; it couldn't be unsaid. Consequently, Lord Coleridge had to ensure somehow that the jury had not taken into account that Mrs Dickman had not given evidence. 'The comment ought to be banished from your minds,' said his lordship, adding pathetically, 'If you have not allowed it to affect your minds you can deliver your verdict.' 'It has not been mentioned,' said the foreman. 'We find him guilty.'

Asked if he had anything to say, Dickman replied, 'I can only repeat that I am entirely innocent of this cruel deed. I have no complicity in this crime and I have spoken the truth in my evidence and in everything I have said.' Lord Coleridge told him, 'In your hungry lust for gold, you had no pity upon the victim whom you slew, and it is only just that the Nemesis of the law should overtake the author of the crime.' Dickman, turning to face the public gallery, then said, 'I declare to all men that I am innocent.'

At the appeal, their lordships heard testimony from Percival Hall about the identification parade, when he had 'picked out' Dickman. It was now that the shameful conduct of the police came to light. Hall said that when he and Spink arrived at the police station they were kept waiting in a passage for ten minutes, then a policeman invited them to look through an internal window. They did so but were unable to see anything. They were then positioned by a door through which policemen continually came and went, and invited to look inside. They saw a man sitting with his back to the door. He wore a light grey overcoat and was hatless. Shortly afterwards, when Hall identified Dickman, did he identify the man he had just seen seated? Hall still maintained he had picked out the right man, but in any event their lordships declared his evidence was 'not important'. Not important! Hall's identification put Dickman as getting onto the train with Nisbet in the very compartment in which Nisbet was murdered.

Dickman's only hope of reprieve lay at the hands of the Home Secretary, who found no grounds to commute the sentence. And so, just before 8 a.m. on Tuesday, 9 August 1910, John Dickman was taken from his cell in Newcastle Prison and pinioned by John Ellis, the hangman. He should then have been taken directly to the gallows. Instead, he declared he was not going to die with his coat on. Removal of the pinioning straps was unprecedented, but seeing 'a nasty gleam in his eye' Ellis removed the straps and permitted Dickman to remove his coat. Dickman then walked calmly to the scaffold – and to his death.

★ ★ ★

There is another matter in connection with John Dickman. Dickman was suspected of the murder of Caroline Mary Luard, near her home at Ightham, Kent, in 1908, although he was never arrested or charged with the crime. Mrs Luard's husband, Major General Charles Edward Luard, late of the Royal Engineers, Justice of the Peace and more, was a personal friend of the judge at Dickman's trial, Lord Coleridge, and every member of the appeal court who upheld Dickman's conviction, and even Winston Churchill, the Home Secretary, who declined to commute his sentence. Was justice done in this case?

The one piece of evidence that convinced the jury that John Dickman was a murderer was surely that of the artist, Wilson Hepple, who saw Dickman standing on the platform at Newcastle Central station, barely twenty feet away. Hanging back before boarding the train, Hepple saw Dickman get into the first carriage of the train with an unknown man. Not a carriage at the back, as Dickman maintained. His testimony was damning; without it Dickman would probably have walked free.

Which leaves one matter unresolved. When Dickman saw Thomas Athey, the ticket collector, then Edwin Elliott and William Sanderson in Morpeth town centre on the day of the crime, it seems certain he was not carrying a bag weighing a stone and a half. So where was the bag? Down the Isabella pitshaft, of course, minus the money. Dickman was arrested just three days after the crime, and was not in possession of the money. So where was the money?

It is conjecture only, but having shot John Nisbet between Stannington and Morpeth, it is submitted here that Dickman threw the bag from the train at a chosen spot, walked back to retrieve it, removed the gold and silver, then threw the bag down the Isabella pitshaft before hiding the loot somewhere in the fields south of Morpeth. If his early arrest prevented him from returning to that hiding place, it may still be there.

Nine

'A LOSS OF MENTAL BALANCE'

Bedlington, 1913

John Vickers Amos – or Jocker, as he was known – left school at twelve and, like many of his Northumbrian peers, went to work down the pit. Unusually for a pitman in the Northumberland coalfield, however, he had ventured to the United States no less than four times to work in the coalmines there. Unfortunately for him, during the latter part of his time in America, he was present during two coal mining tragedies, both caused by explosions due to coal gas below ground.

Both explosions occurred in the summer of 1912. In the first, two men were killed and fourteen, including Amos, received burns. Despite his injuries, he returned to the scene of the blast three times, rescuing two injured miners. Not surprisingly, the effects of the explosion affected his health, when he afterwards suffered from pains in the head, a condition we may today call 'stress'. The second explosion killed eight miners. Many others received burns, although Amos on this occasion was uninjured, physically at least. Nevertheless, his health suffered again through more stress and loss of memory.

Less than six months later, in January 1913, thirty-five-year-old Amos, having returned to England, took up the position as manager of the Sun Inn at Bedlington, a far cry from working down the pit, but in an area he knew well. The inn was owned by James Wood Irons, who lived in Newcastle. The terms of Amos's employment were a salary of thirty shillings (£1.50) a week, plus 5 per cent. On taking up employment Amos had to pay a bond of £30.

On 28 February Irons visited the inn and did a stock check with Amos. The invoices were passed to a stocktaker who noted a shortage of £7 5s 6d. On 16 March there was another deficiency, of £21 11s 3d. Irons spoke to Amos, who told him 'every penny' had been paid. Irons said he wasn't blaming Amos or his wife, but he would have to 'make a

Sun Inn, Bedlington, *c.* 1913. (Reproduced by kind permission of Mr John Reed)

hole' in his £30 bond. When Irons's stocktaker went through the stock again, his statement to Irons showed another deficiency, this time in excess of £17 in just three weeks. The total deficiency was now over £45, which Amos disputed, saying all the takings had been put into the till. Irons then gave Amos notice of dismissal, and approached a Mr Richard Grice to take over the management on 15 April. Due to the shortfall in takings, Irons made it clear Amos would not be getting his £30 bond back.

Whether these shortfalls were the result of Amos's inexperience – he was, after all, a coal miner by trade – or being on the fiddle, which he denied, isn't known. But on 15 April Irons found Amos still on the premises, the latter saying he would not budge until his bond was returned. Irons said he would 'see about that'. Whatever Amos would have ultimately decided to do was then affected by the chance appearance of his wife at the top of the stairs carrying his Winchester rifle, saying a friend wanted to practise shooting with it. Amos told her it was not to be taken out of the house.

Later that morning Irons went to the railway station to collect the new tenants, Mr and Mrs Grice, whom he took to the Sun Inn, even though Amos, his wife and their three children had still not quit the premises. Shortly after noon Amos sent his son, George, to buy a box of cartridges at Joyce the Saddlers, just across the street. Irons, meanwhile, told Mr Grice to take possession of the stock. One can imagine Amos's state of mind: the loss of his £30 and he and his family about to be made homeless – and all after his torrid experiences in America. He stormed upstairs, saying, 'I'll soon let you know who's boss here.' Concerned over Amos's conduct, Irons went to the police station where he was told a constable would be sent to ensure Mr Grice could take over his landlord duties peaceably.

When Irons returned, he and Mr Grice went down into the cellar. Soon after, Irons heard a woman shouting that 'murder was going on upstairs', and he ran up to the smoke room where he saw Mrs Craggs, who was in the premises with some children. She had emerged from the cellar hatchway to face Amos who was pointing the rifle directly at her. She calmly said to him, 'On account of the children do not shoot.' He lowered the gun and allowed them to leave. Irons then went directly to the police station for assistance.

Police Constable George Mussell attended the Sun Inn without delay. He had been in the premises only a few minutes when two shots were heard by a number of people who were gathered outside, including Sergeant Andrew Barton who was standing nearby. Barton went at once to investigate. Then Mrs Grice appeared at an upstairs window of the inn, shouting, 'Hinnies, save me, save me!' Amos then emerged with the rifle, and told the crowd to 'get away' or he would shoot them. 'Don't shoot me, Jocker,' said a man named Wilson. 'Just git,' said Amos. As the crowd backed off Amos aimed the rifle at Mrs Grice at the upstairs window, whereupon she stepped back from sight, her appearance described as being in 'mortal terror'. Amos then went into the building again.

James Corbett had witnessed events and went to the back of the inn. Entering, he found Constable Mussell lying dead in the passage. He came out and saw Amos at the front. Amos said to him, 'Mr Corbett, the man inside has £30 belonging to me and won't give it to me.' He then approached Corbett and said, 'If you come inside I will shoot you.' Mrs Amos was crying but her husband pushed her aside. 'Get away or I'll shoot you all,' he cried, whereupon Sergeant Barton appeared at the gate and told Amos to put down the gun.

'Stop there or I'll shoot,' said Amos, pointing the rifle at the policeman. Undaunted, Sergeant Barton told him to put down the gun and took a step forward. Amos, standing only three yards away, shot him the chest. Thomas Wilson witnessed the shooting: 'He staggered on his left leg and when his back was turned Amos stepped forward and fired another shot at him.'

Outside again, Amos threatened to shoot anyone who challenged him. He then calmly placed the rifle onto the ground and lit a cigarette, before putting the rifle to his head and shouting, 'I still have two cartridges, one for that ★★★★ [expletive unknown, but meaning Irons] and I am keeping the other for myself.'

Someone went to the police station where Inspector Culley, 'realising the seriousness of the situation', telephoned other police stations for assistance, and a standoff prevailed until the arrival of police officers from other districts. They included the Chief Constable, Captain Fullarton James, and Superintendents Marshall and Tough. Other officers arrived on bicycles. On sight of the approaching police, Amos discharged his rifle at no one in particular before fleeing through the back door to the open fields beyond.

The police wasted no time in throwing a cordon around the fields. Some were armed with revolvers, as were some civilians who volunteered to help in the search. With darkness approaching it seemed Amos might have escaped. But then, three hours after the tragic events at the inn, Inspector Hutchinson was directed to a sewer that ran under Church Lane, about 400 yards from the inn. He saw that there was a culvert some fifteen yards long and two feet in diameter that led to the sewer, and noticed footprints near the entrance. He asked a miner named Potter, who had a gun, to fire a shot into the culvert, which he did. There was then 'a noise', but Amos did not appear. 'Fire another shot,' the inspector

Police Constable George Mussell. (Reproduced by kind permission of Mr John Reed)

Sergeant Andrew Barton. (Reproduced by kind permission of Mr John Reed)

Mrs Elizabeth Grice. (Reproduced by kind permission of Mr John Reed)

told Potter. When he did Amos cried out in pain and appeared immediately afterwards, bleeding from injuries to his head. He held his hands up and was arrested by PC Smith. The rifle was retrieved from the culvert.

Amos, all bloodied, was marched to the police station, followed by a procession of police and hundreds of men, women and children. Not surprisingly, he required medical attention for gunshot wounds caused by pellets, but his injuries were not serious. Later, when his gun was examined, a cartridge was found in the barrel but it seems the gun had jammed, possibly in an attempt by Amos to take his own life.

That afternoon a doctor was called to the Sun Inn where he examined three bodies. The first was of Constable Mussell, who was lying on his back in a pool of blood near the door, still wearing his helmet. There was a large wound on right side of his neck and lower jaw, exposing the jugular veins and other 'chief vessels'. There was another gunshot wound extending to the shoulder bone.

In the kitchen was the body of Sergeant Barton. He lay on his back in a pool of blood, his head against the pantry door. He was still breathing, but a gunshot wound to his chest 'was mortal', the bullet having penetrated the heart. Mrs Grice lay on the cellar floor. She had been shot at the top of the cellar stairs. She too was breathing, and she was carried up to the bar where she died. She had been shot through the head, and had suffered a fractured skull, probably through tumbling down the staircase.

These events at a small tavern in Bedlington on an April day in 1913 amounted to one of the greatest tragedies ever in Northumberland. Two policemen shot dead in the course of their duty; the wife of a man newly appointed as manager shot in cold blood in a place she had just began to call her home. Both policemen were, of course, unarmed. Constable Mussell was thirty-two, a married man. Sergeant Barton, too, was married, and had two sons. The police authority only had the power to grant £15 per annum to their widows, plus £2 10s to each child up to the age of fifteen.

Both officers knew that Amos was in possession of a firearm and acted with commendable courage. In the case of Sergeant Barton, he went into the premises knowing shots had been fired. His actions were hardly a surprise; he had once risked his life by diving into stormy seas off Warkworth to rescue a boy who was lashed to the mast of a stricken ship. Amos, whatever his state of mind when he shot the policemen, could have had no cause to shoot Mrs Grice, who would only have wanted to be allowed to leave the premises. Yet he was a man who ordinarily would never have offered violence to anyone. A local businessman, Alderman Fairbairn told the *Morpeth Herald and Reporter* that Amos, whom he knew, was 'a very quiet man who attended well to his business'.

Amos appeared before the magistrates at Bedlington the following day, his head swathed in bandages. He was formally charged with three murders. The two murdered policemen were buried in Bedlington cemetery, on the 'saddest day in which they had ever met,' said the vicar.

The inquest into all three deaths was heard at Bedlington Courthouse before the coroner, Mr Rutherford. After hearing the testimony of witnesses, including the doctor, the coroner had two questions for the jury: 'Are you satisfied that these persons died from the wounds described by the doctor?' – a matter he said he thought they would have no difficulty with; and 'Who do you think inflicted these wounds?' The jury took ten minutes to return verdicts of wilful murder by Amos, who was remanded to the assizes to stand trial.

Mr Potter with his shotgun: the man who shot Jocker Amos. (Reproduced by kind permission of Mr John Reed)

Jocker Amos in court. Evidence of the head wounds he received after being shot is clearly visible, if one looks at his bandaged head. (Reproduced by kind permission of Mr John Reed)

John Vickers Amos appeared at the Summer Assizes, Newcastle, in July. Although the names of the three murdered people appeared on the indictment, the jury would be concerned with only one: Sergeant Andrew Barton. Commissioner English Harrison presided. Prosecution counsel was led by Mr Bruce Williamson, the defence by Mr W.J. Waugh. Amos, who had been incarcerated in Newcastle Prison, had but a short distance to travel, to the Moot Hall, to stand trial for his life. He pleaded not guilty.

Mr Williamson told the jury Amos had 'taken the life of Sergeant Barton deliberately and intentionally, knowing what he was doing'. There was no medical evidence to consider, other than that of the doctor who saw Amos immediately after the events in the Sun Inn and who described him then as 'quiet, collected and perfectly composed'. Referring to the incident when Amos had lowered the gun to allow Mrs Craggs and the children to pass unharmed, Mr Williamson said this tended to show 'he was in such a condition of mind, he appreciated Mrs Craggs's appeal and acted upon it'. He shot the officer because he wanted to keep the gun, and all the evidence 'pointed to his having a rational mind'.

Mr Waugh said the only thing the jury had to consider was the state of Amos's mind when he shot Sergeant Barton. 'Amos's conduct on the fatal day was the strongest evidence that his mind was not the mind of the prisoner today.' He referred to the 'marked change' in him between the time he went to America and when he came back to England. Testifying in his own defence, Amos said he never took stock, but left it to Mr Irons. He said that when at the Sun Inn he raised the takings from £10 a week to £26 a week. He said during the row [on 15 April] Irons had threatened to cut his throat and said he would not 'get a halfpenny' of his bond back. He recalled nothing after that until he appeared in the magistrates' court the following day. He had no grievance against any of the dead, but said 'that man Irons drove me wild'.

Mr Waugh said Mr Irons had driven a 'hard bargain' with Amos. The price Irons put on a barrel of beer meant the manager was bound to show a deficiency in stock. It was impossible for anyone, however diligent, however honest he might be, to comply with the terms Mr Irons laid down, namely that Amos was to be charged seventy shillings for every barrel. Mr Irons was getting it both ways, said Mr Waugh: the bigger the turnover, the bigger the deficit – the tenant after Amos was showing a stock deficiency of £1 a day. Amos had been through the rough experiences of coalmines in America, which had been a terrible strain on his mental faculties. 'If only his wife hadn't appeared with the gun,' said Mr Waugh. 'It might have been the sight of it that put something into his head, a subconscious motive that otherwise would never have been there.' He might have added how deplorable it was that Amos was able to send his young son on an errand to buy ammunition.

Mr Waugh said it was Mr Irons that Amos had wanted to harm. Not the two policemen, not Mrs Grice – 'What possible reason could he have for killing that unfortunate woman? … Was his conduct that of a sane man? … Don't you think he was mad at the time? … So mad he did not care what he did? He was prepared to kill anybody because he had lost his mental balance. His reason had been dethroned.' He said Amos was temporarily insane and not responsible for his 'extraordinary deeds'.

The judge said that if Amos was not insane, the killing of Sergeant Barton was murder. The presumption of the law was that every man was responsible for his own acts. The jury had to consider whether Amos was suffering from a defect of reason so that he didn't know what the nature of his acts was. Was the forfeiture of the £30

Jocker Amos. (Reproduced by kind permission of Mr John Reed

deposit sufficient to unhinge a man's mind to the extent that the law required it to unhinge (before killing someone)? No medical person had testified about what effects the two explosions in America had had on Amos's mind. They only had the statement of Amos himself that he didn't know what he was doing. The jury must not be guided by sympathy, but by sense of duty. The jury returned after eight minutes, their verdict: 'Guilty of wilful murder.' When asked what he had to say, Amos replied, 'I don't remember anything. They were good friends of mine.'

His lordship said, 'You have been convicted of the cruel murder of a police sergeant who appears to have given to his important duties and executed them with zeal and discretion, as well as courage. Your crime is aggravated by the additional killing of Constable Mussell and Mrs Grice.' He sentenced Amos to death.

★ ★ ★

If the trial was over, the issue wasn't.

A petition signed by 60,651 people was sent to the Home Secretary, urging him to commute the death sentence. When, at the Northumberland Miners' Picnic at Morpeth, attended by thousands of miners and their wives and children, a resolution was passed calling for the Home Secretary to show mercy, the *Blyth News and Telegraph* reported that 'not a single hand was raised against it'. Hundreds of miners knew Amos. They considered him to be a respectable man who had always worked hard. They knew of the tragedies in America, that he had saved lives and had been affected mentally; they believed his mental balance was impaired at the Sun Inn that day. But there would be no reprieve, and when he was told Amos issued a statement thanking all who had signed the petition for their efforts. He also thanked the governor and staff of Newcastle gaol, saying, 'I have been treated throughout like a gentleman.'

On 22 July 1913, 'a cold, cheerless morn', over a thousand people waited outside Newcastle Prison as the hour of execution approached. Jocker Amos rose early and after prayers and a light breakfast he was taken to the gallows. The hangman was Thomas Pierrepoint. Amos stood on the trapdoor without hesitation, allowing Pierrepoint to place the white cap over his head and draw the bolt. The Under-Sheriff, Percy Corder, reported that Amos met his death 'very bravely'. He died at eight o'clock precisely, just as the cathedral clock chimed the hour.

But did Amos's mental condition play a meaningful part in his actions on the day he killed three people? Why wasn't a report concerning his mental condition available at his trial? It is beyond dispute that he returned from America unwell through tragic events there; it is beyond dispute that he was being given notice to quit his home and place of work by a man whom he said 'drove him wild'. Many believed, and who could say otherwise, that the £30 bond – a considerable sum – had always been coveted by Irons, whose intention had always been to keep the bond, using Amos's alleged shortfall in takings as an excuse to sack him. A coalminer, inexperienced in stocktaking, Amos may well have been short in the till, but he would have considered himself honest. The forfeit of his bond could not in itself be reason to kill someone; but 'reason' was probably something not featuring in John Vickers Amos's mind that day.

Memorial to the murdered policemen, Bedlington cemetery. (© Paul Heslop, 2011)

Ten

A VERDICT OF MURDER

Otterburn, 1931

It was Tuesday 6 January, a cold winter's evening. Cecil Johnson, driving the last bus from Newcastle to Otterburn, would hardly have expected anything out of the ordinary on the lonely road crossing the wild moors of Northumberland. Indeed, by the time the bus reached Knowesgate, near Kirkwhelpington, it was empty, and for Johnson and his conductor, Tommy Rutherford, it was just a matter of completing what would surely be an uneventful journey.

But it was not uneventful, for at about ten o'clock, as the bus approached the moorland wilderness known as Wolf's Nick on the Ottercaps, Johnson and Rutherford noticed a car on fire on the moor. After stopping and approaching it on foot, they recognised it as belonging to their employer's daughter, Miss Evelyn Foster. Then, in the darkness, as they were close to the vehicle, they heard moans, and, whilst searching, they came upon an object which they discovered to be Evelyn herself. She was lying on the frozen moor, muttering repeatedly, 'That awful man …'

Evelyn had lain on the ground suffering from appalling injuries for about an hour and a half. The front, lower half of her body was badly burnt; she was naked from the waist down, her clothing charred and in remnants.

As Cecil Johnson carried her to the bus, she kept repeating, 'That awful man'. Johnson then made haste for Otterburn. On that wintry night it must have seemed an eternity before they reached the village, where they took Evelyn directly to her home, the Kennels. Her brother, Gordon, sent for blankets and the police were called. Evelyn was still conscious and when her mother, Margaret, asked her what had happened, she replied, 'Oh, it has been that man. He hit me and burned me.'

Evelyn Foster lived with her parents. She ran a hire car business from the Foster's garage at Otterburn, and that evening, just after 6.30, she had taken a fare to Low Byrness, near

Cecil Johnson, bus driver. (Author's colection)

Tommy Rutherford, bus conductor. (Author's collection)

Rochester. At 7 p.m. she came home and told her parents that on the way back from Low Byrness, at Elishaw, where the main road is joined by the Hexham road (the A68), she was flagged down by some people who told her they were going to Hexham, but a man they'd given a lift to at Jedburgh wanted to go to Newcastle. The man asked Evelyn to take him to Ponteland, where he hoped to catch a bus the rest of the way to Newcastle.

Evelyn described the man to her mother as 'very respectable and gentlemanly-like; he looked a bit of a knut [a crazy person]'. She had left to take the man to Ponteland in her car, a Hudson Super Six. The man was clean-shaven, and wore a bowler hat and dark overcoat. 'He hit me and burned me,' she said.

There was no further conversation until the arrival of Dr McEachran and a nurse, and Police Constable Andrew Ferguson. Evelyn, despite being in excruciating pain, was able to give them her account of events. She said that having picked up the strange man at Elishaw, when she arrived at Otterburn, on the way to Ponteland, she called home to fill the car with petrol, whilst the man said he would pop into the Percy Arms in the village. She said that as she had driven through Belsay the man said they would turn around, and she felt him 'creep along the seat towards her'. He took hold of the steering wheel and said he would drive. When she said she would do the driving he hit her over the eye. The man then drove north, and when they reached Wolf's Nick he 'knocked her into the back of the car' and 'interfered' with her. He then took something from his pocket and threw it over her and 'it went up in a blaze'.

Evelyn said that after the car had been set on fire on the moor she'd heard a car pull up and someone whistling. She was sitting in the back of the car when she had been set on fire, and was choking on fumes when she scrambled out. She crawled as far as she could then lay still, waiting for help, pressing her burnt face and body into the cold ground. She was 'completely lucid', and drifted in and out of consciousness throughout the night. During one short period of consciousness she said, 'Mother, I have been murdered.' She died at 7.30 the following morning.

Not surprisingly a hue and cry went up throughout the border country, where people were shocked and dismayed at such a brutal attack. The police cast their net far and wide, searching for the mysterious stranger. Their efforts, which included an appeal on BBC radio, were in vain: no one reported seeing a mystery-man; no one came forward to say they had dropped a man at Elishaw. Their only success was to recover some of Evelyn's clothing at the scene of the attack: her scarf, a glove and her slightly-burnt handbag which still contained money.

An inquest into Evelyn's death was opened in the Memorial Hall, Otterburn. The coroner was Mr Philip Dodds. After formal identification, the inquest was adjourned until 2 February. When it took place events proved to be quite sensational when Professor Stuart MacDonald said he did not consider Evelyn had been attacked at all, and implied that she was responsible for her own death. MacDonald, who carried out the post-mortem examination on Evelyn's body, declared there was no trace of any injury to her face, nor of 'violation' – that she had been raped – saying implicitly that she was a virgin – and further that it was possible that if she had poured petrol on her car she could have 'splashed some on herself', and it may have become ignited.

Miss Evelyn Foster. (Courtesy of Solo Syndication Ltd)

Mr Foster, Evelyn's father, said he last saw his daughter at 7.10 p.m., when she called at Otterburn to fill up with petrol. They had no conversation about the man she allegedly had picked up, now apparently waiting somewhere in the village. He confirmed the car was Evelyn's. It had a luggage box on the back that was never locked and contained a two-gallon petrol can, kept in the carrier, for use in an emergency. Evelyn had bought the car for £200 fourteen months before and it was insured for £450.

Other witnesses included John Kennedy, a road repair man, who said on the evening of the tragedy he was at Kirkwhelpington. At about 8 p.m., as he was walking home, a car overtook him, heading north towards Wolf's Nick. A man was driving. He saw no one else in the vehicle. What he didn't say at the inquest, but apparently did later to the police, was that the number plate contained the figures '13'. The number of Evelyn's car was TN 8135.

Gordon Foster, Evelyn's brother, was asked by the police to take a lorry to Wolf's Nick and remove the burnt-out car, which he did. He said he had seen Evelyn before she took her initial fare to High Rochester; the next time he saw her was when she was brought home on the bus when he asked her what had happened. 'Who has done this? Has it been that man you took from here to Ponteland?' 'Yes Gordon,' she replied, 'he burnt me and the car.'

PC Ferguson gave evidence of Evelyn's story as she related it to him, and quoted her as saying, 'He was too strong for me. He set the car on fire. My eyes were sore with him striking me. I heard a car pull up and someone whistle while the car was on fire. I was choking with the fumes when I got out.' The constable said he went to the scene of the fire where 'various articles' were found, including a petrol can on the car carrier, an empty bottle and Evelyn's purse, and that with other officers he later 'scoured the neighbourhood'. Inspector Russell of Prudhoe went to Wolf's Nick. He described the position of the car on the moor, and how he traced its line of travel from the road. The car was burnt out except for the engine and front. He produced some items of clothing that were found on the nearside of the car, and some 'burnt articles' which were given to Professor MacDonald.

Mr Foster was recalled and asked about Evelyn's 'earnings'. He had no idea, he said, as the records were destroyed in the car. 'She would hardly carry her account book there,' said the coroner. 'It has been burnt in the car,' was all Mr Foster could say. 'Can you at least give us her bank balance?' the coroner asked. Foster handed him a document, saying, 'This is from her bank, Lloyds at Bellingham.' The coroner read out the figure as £489 10s. When Foster was asked about 'insurance' he produced two insurance policies. One was for the car being insured for £450. 'It appears to cover risk only whilst in the garage,' the coroner remarked, adding that it was in Mr Foster's name, not Evelyn's. 'We have a floating policy with the insurance people and get it a cheaper rate,' Mr Foster replied. The second policy insured any car up to 30 horsepower driven by Mr Foster against fire, theft or accident on the road up to £700, the amount payable depending on the current value of the car.

Professor MacDonald, giving details of the post-mortem examination, said that Evelyn was burnt most severely on the front of the middle part of the body – the upper thighs and lower abdomen. Her face had superficial burns. There was no evidence of 'violation', nor of assault. He concluded:

From these appearances we are of the opinion that the cause of death was shock, the result of severe external burning … The distribution of the burns and their severity in certain places suggested that certain portions of the clothing had contained some inflammable substance, and that burning had started in front and was most severe on the upper and inner aspects of the thighs, and generally appeared diminishing in intensity in an upward and downward direction … The distribution of the burnt areas on the lower portion of the buttocks and the absence of burning on the upper portion of the buttocks suggested that the girl had been sitting during some period of the burning … the absence of burning on the upper part of the chest and the chin might be accounted for by the bending forward of the body.

He had found no evidence of severe blows.

The coroner related to the professor Evelyn's story, that a man had assaulted her, thrown her over the back seat of the car and thrown something over her, and that she remembered nothing more until she was awakened by bumping (the car crossing the moor). Could Professor MacDonald tell by her burns if she had been sitting or lying in the back seat? 'It is possible,' McDonald replied. William Jennings, a motor engineer, said the fire had occurred after the car had got on to the moor.

Summing up, the coroner said there were two main points for the jury to consider. Was Evelyn murdered? Or did she set fire to the car and obtain the burns accidentally? If there was a man, he said, he was either a homicidal maniac or had something to hide. If Evelyn had set fire to the car, the jury had to consider what her object might be. To obtain insurance money, he ventured. Concluding, he added:

My opinion is that I do not think there is sufficient evidence to say that these burns were caused by another person. However, it is for you to say, but it will be improper to say these burns were caused by another person unless you are absolutely certain they were so caused … If you cannot come to a decision as to how the burns were caused it is open to you to say you consider there is not sufficient evidence to say definitely how they were caused.

Miss Foster's burnt-out Humber car in-situ on the moors. (Courtesy of Solo Syndication Ltd)

Having been virtually directed to return a verdict of 'accident' or 'misadventure', the jury, after two hours' deliberation, unanimously stated that, 'We find that Evelyn Foster died on the 7th day of January 1931 at the Kennels, Otterburn, from shock due to burns caused by petrol being wilfully thrown over her and ignited by some person or persons unknown.' The jury, despite the obvious opinion of the police and Professor MacDonald, and even the coroner, had decided Evelyn Foster had been murdered. Notwithstanding this, a few days later the Chief Constable, Captain Fullarton James, told a national newspaper, 'We are satisfied that the man she described does not exist.'

If such an assertion by a policeman after the lawful verdict of an inquest jury was surprising, the content of a letter written to the Home Secretary by Evelyn's father was hardly surprising at all. 'Many painful and scandalous innuendos against my daughter's character were made during the inquest,' he wrote, adding that 'it was even suggested that she fired the car herself to obtain the insurance money …' He pointed out that it had been suggested that Evelyn had set fire to the car to gain notoriety for herself. 'There was no evidence to support these shameful theories … the jury's verdict vindicated my girl's integrity.'

Alluding to the Chief Constable's 'statement', he wrote:

I resent the police force covering its own failures through a veiled and uncalled for attack on my dead daughter … I hope and pray you will devote your attention in conjunction with the following questions:

1. Was my daughter's burned car left unprotected for hours so that fingerprints could not be taken?
2. Is it a fact that the police made no attempt to check footprints at the scene of the tragedy until the ground had been trampled over by curious sightseers?
3. Why was the skill and experience of Scotland Yard ignored by the Northumberland Police?'

It is submitted here that these were fair questions, one and all.

Today, the scene at Wolf's Nick would be cordoned off, with no one permitted to encroach upon it, including police officers other than those directly engaged, so that it could be examined for evidence by trained forensic personnel. The scene at Wolf's Nick was treated very differently, with policemen walking all over it, in darkness as well as daylight, randomly picking up items and perhaps destroying evidence such as footprints. Curious sightseers also ventured on to the location. The car was, presumably, checked for fingerprints, successfully or otherwise, we do not know. As for the skill and experience of Scotland Yard, it was practice then to call in the 'Yard' for murder cases. Not because policemen from London had better minds than policemen in the provinces, but because they were trained detectives. Northumberland County Constabulary had no Criminal Investigation Department in 1931. However, in this case, the police decided there had been no crime in the first place.

The police were unable to trace anyone who had given a man a lift from Jedburgh to Elishaw, or the man himself, Evelyn's alleged attacker. The man, according to Evelyn, had said he would pop into the Percy Arms while she filled up with petrol, but enquiries there were negative when one might have expected a stranger to be readily remembered in such a small village. Then again he may not have called there at all. Evelyn said the man

Evelyn Foster's grave, Otterburn churchyard. (© Paul Heslop, 2011)

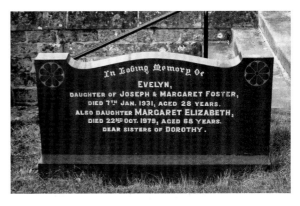

'took something from his pocket and threw it over her and it went up in a blaze'; an empty bottle was found on the moor. Was it examined for fingerprints? Other than the flimsy suggestion that the number '13' appeared in the number plate of a car seen travelling north towards Wolf's Nick by John Kennedy, the roadman, there seemed little else to support what Evelyn said.

We are left to consider motive. Evelyn Foster was a respectable young woman who had established her own car hire business. The coroner, clearly believing 'insurance fraud' had been attempted, questioned her father about car insurance and Evelyn's finances. (Such questions were surely a matter for the police.) Notwithstanding the 'amount insured', £700 maximum, the amount she would have been able to claim was dependant on the car's current value, probably less than £100. She had £489 10s in the bank – a healthy sum then – as well as other disposable assets.

Then we have her injuries. There were burns to her buttocks, hardly consistent with injuries sustained by someone standing outside the car throwing petrol over it. She stated clearly that the man had thrown her into the back of the car. Professor MacDonald agreed it was 'possible' she was sitting or lying on the back seat. From his own testimony: 'The distribution of the burnt areas on the lower portion of the buttocks and the absence of burning on the upper portion of the buttocks suggested that the girl had been sitting during some period of the burning.' She alleged the man had 'interfered' with her; MacDonald said she was still a virgin, meaning she had not been raped. But by 'interfered' she may have meant a sexual assault short of rape. Finally, Evelyn Foster knew she was dying: 'Mother I have been murdered.' Believing this, would she have concocted a story about a strange man? There is much to suggest what she said was the truth.

No arrest was ever made in connection with the death of Evelyn Foster, but the case of one Ernest Brown was considered by many to be interesting. Brown, thirty-one, was employed as a stable groom on a farm near Tadcaster. In 1933 he shot and killed his employer – the men had quarrelled over Brown's liaison with his employer's wife – and tried to cremate his body in a blazing garage. A native of Newcastle, Brown's description matched that given by Evelyn of the man she said had attacked her, and he could drive, as not everyone could in the 1930s. Brown travelled throughout the north of England attending horse fairs. Most telling, perhaps, was that on the scaffold, just prior to his execution in February 1934, when asked to confess, he allegedly said 'Otterburn', or perhaps, 'Ought to burn.' Unfortunately the hangman pulled the lever without asking him to explain what he meant. Had he done so there may yet have been a definite conclusion into the tragic death of Evelyn Foster.

Eleven

'WITH MALICE AFORETHOUGHT'

Newcastle, 1942

It was a fine summer's morning, and John Jones, a milkman with the Co-op, had just about finished his round. It was 8.30 a.m. on Saturday, 13 June 1942, and Jones would have been looking forward to getting home for his breakfast in wartime Britain. He was in Claremont Road, Newcastle, a street lined with houses on one side only, the other open land leading onto the Town Moor, a scene largely unchanged today. Some large, black pipes lay on the grass by the side of the road, ready for workmen to lay them in the ground, and as he passed them Jones spotted something lying partly concealed behind one of the pipes.

Jones crossed the road and was horrified at what he saw. There, on the grass, was the body of a young woman. She lay on her back, naked from the waist down, her upper clothing pushed high on her torso, revealing her breasts. Some of her clothing, including her underwear, was strewn about the ground nearby. There was blood on her head and face, and Jones could not have been in any doubt that she was dead. He contacted the police immediately.

The police officers attending the gruesome scene would have known at once they were dealing with a murder, accompanied by a frenzied sexual assault. That same afternoon Dr George Stephenson conducted a post-mortem examination and found marks of bruising about the woman's neck, consistent with strangulation; but the cause of death was fourteen wounds to the head, several penetrating to the bone, and the skull was fractured. He concluded she had been battered with an instrument and held down by the throat. The *Evening Chronicle* reported: 'The murder is the act of a sex maniac, robbery being

incidental'. The newspaper went on to warn 'any females who may have recently been frightened by the approaches of suspicious men to apply descriptions'.

The dead woman was twenty-four-year-old Mrs Margaret Mary Rice, a serving WAAF corporal, stationed at The Uplands, Kenton. She was wearing a two-piece black and grey costume, and was smartly dressed. A native of Epping, Mrs Rice was recently married, on 21 April, to Lieutenant Patrick Leslie Rice, RA, based at Woolwich, London. Lieutenant Rice had been granted leave and had travelled to Newcastle to see his wife. He left Newcastle less than forty-eight hours later on the one o'clock train for London on the very morning his wife's body was discovered. She had seen him off at Newcastle Central station, before setting off to walk to Kenton. Significantly, her husband had given her an Irish threepenny piece as a good luck charm.

When found dead, Mrs Rice was wearing a gold bangle, a gold necklace with a stone pendant and a Royal Artillery brooch in her coat lapel. However, some property was missing, believed stolen by her attacker, including the threepenny piece, a 22-carat plain gold wedding ring, a gold dress ring set with two diamonds and a blue sapphire in the centre, a plain metal bangle, the colour of tarnished silver, her purse and contents, including her keys and some money, a Royal Air Force pass and identity card. No obvious murder weapon was found at the scene, but the police did find 'two clues', as the *Chronicle* described them, adding that 'the nature of these clues cannot be divulged'.

Central railway station, Newcastle. (© Paul Heslop, 2011)

It seemed likely that Mrs Rice had been murdered as she walked home after seeing her husband off from Newcastle Central station, which would probably put the time of death about 2 a.m. The police quickly put up a reward of £100 for information that would lead to the arrest and conviction of the murderer. The *Chronicle*, meanwhile, reported that 'any man observed lurking in the vicinity of Claremont Road should be regarded as a suspect and information should be given to the police immediately'. Such a man might have attracted attention by bloodstains on his person or clothing, or by his confused behaviour, said the newspaper.

On the face of it, the police would have a difficult task in tracing and identifying the culprit, but an unexpected development quickly assisted them in their endeavours. It occurred at 6.45 p.m. on the day Margaret Rice's body was found, when a twenty-one-year-old man came forward with some information. He was William Ambrose Collins, a merchant navy apprentice who lived with his mother in Framlington Place, near Claremont Road.

Collins said he had gone to the nearby Royal Oak public house about 7 p.m. the previous evening, and there met a friend, Eddie Morgan. After a few drinks and a game of darts, the pair left together in Morgan's car at about 8.30 and went to the Travellers Rest on the Great North Road at Wideopen, where they drank until closing time at ten o'clock. From there, they went to a dance at Seaton Burn, leaving at 12.40 on the Saturday morning, when they went to the Central station where they had pie and lemonade. About half an hour later they left, Morgan dropping Collins off near his home at the corner of Claremont Road and Park Terrace. Collins said he didn't notice a woman in that area, although he did see a man riding a bicycle heading in the direction of the Haymarket.

The police thanked Collins for the information, before allowing him to go on his way. They could not have known at that time that the two clues found at the scene could be connected to him. These were two small pieces of vulcanite, a hard, rubber-like substance, found on the grass verge near to Mrs Rice's body. They were part of the butt of a revolver, which may have been the weapon used to cause the injuries to Mrs Rice's head. It was obvious if the police could find the gun they would be a long way to identifying the murderer. The man who would lead them to find it was none other than the man Collins had been with the previous evening.

Edward Bircham Morgan, a motor salesman, lived at Burdon Terrace, Jesmond. Morgan told the police that on 11 June, two days before the crime, he agreed to sell Collins a Webley revolver for thirty shillings. The following evening, when they met at the Royal Oak, as Collins had said, Morgan sold Collins the revolver, but no ammunition. They then went to the Travellers Rest and then to the dance at Seaton Burn in his, Morgan's, car. Although they had drank six half pints of alcohol at the Travellers Rest, alcohol was not available at the dance. Collins was quite sober, said Morgan, who also confirmed their visit to the Central station was alcohol-free, before dropping Collins hear his home.

At 6.20 p.m. on Monday, as Collins was making his way home for tea, the police were waiting. They asked him to accompany them to the police station where, on being searched, an Irish threepenny piece was found in his pocket. He was asked to make a written statement, which he did. In it, he gave the same account as before concerning his movements on Friday night through to Saturday morning, which included his friend, Eddie Morgan, although he said nothing about buying the revolver. Knowing now about Morgan's sale of the gun to him, and the circumstantial evidence of the threepenny piece, the police charged him with the murder. The evidence, to say the least, was tenuous at that point, but the police clearly considered it was sufficient to charge him, as the law required.

It wasn't long before Collins himself provided further evidence to support the charge, for when he was being placed into a cell he asked if he could 'have a word' with the officer in the case, saying that he would like to make an alteration to his statement. Superintendent Weir and Inspector Smith went to the cell and enquired of Collins what he wanted to say. Collins, shrewd enough to foresee the consequences of the wording of the charge, that he 'feloniously, wilfully and with malice aforethought, did kill and murder Margaret Mary Rice', stated the charge was incorrect as there had been no 'aforethought'. Accordingly he wished to make a new statement.

Collins's assertion, that there was no 'aforethought', was tantamount to an admission that he had killed Mrs Rice, except he'd had no 'aforethought' in doing so. In his new statement, he said he had arranged to buy the gun from Eddie Morgan on the Thursday, but, not having the money at that time, the following day he had visited his solicitor and drawn £5 due to him through his grandfather's will, which he used to pay for his night out and the gun. He agreed he'd paid thirty shillings for the gun, a .45 Webley revolver, and that no ammunition had been purchased.

He said that when Morgan dropped him off on the night in question, a young woman walked by and although he could not recall what happened exactly he 'must have hit her with the butt of the revolver'. They struggled and he grabbed her wallet, which he dropped down a drain on the way home. He also took 'some trinkets' and other property from her: a bangle, a handkerchief, a purse, all of which he pushed down drains in the locality of his home. Then, taking a torch, he returned to the scene of the crime', where he saw the woman was 'in a bad way', and that she was stripped below the waist, although he could not recall being responsible. He then took her rings. The following day, as news of the murder spread, he pushed more items down drains. The gun he said he had wiped clean and placed it under his pillow. But, as he had explained, all this was done without 'aforethought'.

The next morning the police went to Collins's home where, underneath his pillow, just as Collins had said, Detective Sergeant William Checkley found the gun. The vulcanite grip was broken, but pieces of it were found in his bedroom and when assembled with the two broken pieces found at the scene of the crime, they formed a perfect handle.

★ ★ ★

William Ambrose Collins stood trial for murder at Newcastle Assizes in August. Justice Cassells presided. Collins pleaded not guilty. There could be no doubt that he was responsible for killing Mrs Rice. If the evidence of finding the gun and the broken parts of the butt, and the discovery of the Irish threepenny bit on his person, were not sufficient, there was other evidence too: council workers, searching the drains in North Terrace near Collins's home, found a comb and a bracelet, and a handkerchief and a powder compact, placed there just as Collins described and all identified as belonging to Margaret Rice; part of the butt of the gun was bloodstained, and the blood, when analysed at the forensic science laboratory, was proved to be human and of Type 'O', the same blood group as Mrs Rice; some of Collins's clothes, recovered from his home, were also was bloodstained with the same blood-type; and there was semen on the trousers and underpants he admitted he had worn on the night in question.

Collins had indeed killed Mrs Rice; but had he murdered her? Was he insane; or was there, as he asserted, no 'malice aforethought'? Men of the medical profession would have something to say in this regard.

Dr B.G. Derry, Medical Officer at Durham Prison, said that since Collins's admission to the prison he had interviewed Collins eight times, 'from the point of view of considering his mental condition'. He had found no symptoms of epilepsy or insanity. He said alcohol, even in small quantities, might have 'striking effects' on a mind susceptible to its influence, and result in acts of violence. During such frenzy, said Dr Derry, a person committing such acts might be unconscious of what he was doing. But, he added, attacks of frenzy from drinking were 'very rare'; he would not expect a young man accustomed to drinking beer to get into a frenzy three and half hours after his last glass. He concluded by saying that Collins's mother had told him a paternal grand-uncle of her son was an imbecile.

Harvey Robson, defending, called Dr Arthur Pool, Physician Superintendent of The Retreat, York, a hospital for nervous and mental illness, who had interviewed Collins the previous Tuesday. Pool had concluded that the frenzy described in the evidence 'would be due to the sudden onset of an attack of *mania a potu*' – madness induced by drinking alcohol. Frenzy was an overt physical act, the result of an excessive emotional reaction of anger, which resulted from 'thwarted instinctive desire produced by a nervous system sensitised by head injury, sunstroke, fever or repeated doses of alcohol'. He referred to a bicycle accident Collins had had four years before, when he had sustained a blow to the head and had suffered from concussion and loss of memory, which could make him super-sensitive to the effects of alcohol. Paley Scott, prosecuting, asked Dr Pool: 'Would he [Collins] subconsciously take off her shoes, underclothes and clothes?'

The Moot Hall, Newcastle, the former assize court. (© Paul Heslop, 2011)

'I think such actions are possible,' replied Dr Pool.

Paley Scott said Dr Pool's evidence was 'a very far-fetched theoretical explanation'. 'I don't know what experience the doctor of a Quaker Mental Hospital may have been of the effects of alcoholic drink, but you might think a doctor who has been in charge for years of one of His Majesty's prisons is likely to have considerable experience of matters like that.' He added that 'not to be in your normal senses' fell far short of what the defence had to prove to satisfy the jury that Collins, when he committed violence, did not know he was committing it; or if he did know he was committing it, he did not know he was doing anything wrong.

Justice Cassells told the jury the defence had set out to prove there was a blank in Collins's mind that caused him, unknowingly or subconsciously, to 'attack that young woman and batter her to death with that revolver,' and that 'when he was doing it he did not know what he was doing.' But, he said, unless it was proved that at the time he committed the act Collins was insane, as the criminal law understood it, his defence was 'not made out'.

'You may think,' said his lordship, 'that the observation was made that some men may get angry if their lustful desire is thwarted or obstructed or resisted, and anger may lead to violence and a lack of self control; but when you reflect upon unfulfilled desires leading to anger, and then to violence which does not cease until death has taken place, you have to ask yourselves: "Are you in the realm of insanity?" ' He went on, 'Is a man entitled to say, "I was resisted. I was angry. I lost control of myself. I killed, but I must be excused because I was in a condition of extreme excitement due to pathological intoxication, and I was a susceptible individual and I didn't know what I was doing?" The mere fact that Collins did this in anger, that perhaps a reasonable man would not do such a thing – are not considerations which should deter you from saying that this man is guilty.'

The jury, presumably having considered that Collins's paternal grand-uncle was an imbecile and what effect, if any, his bicycle accident might have had on him, found Collins guilty as charged. The judge, 'visibly affected by his stern duty', told Collins that, in his view, he had been 'rightly convicted'. 'It was a wicked crime that you committed that night in taking the life of that young woman because she resisted and struggled with you and would not let you have your desire.' Sentencing him to death, he asked him if he had anything to say. Collins, appearing calm and, flinching slightly, said nothing.

Margaret Mary Rice was in her prime, a newly-married woman who was returning to her billet after seeing her husband off on his train. As a couple they would have hoped to survive the war; he, serving in the Royal Artillery, would have expected his life to be most at risk. In the event she was to die, not in service of her country, but at the hands of a brutal killer. William Ambrose Collins was hanged at Durham Prison by Thomas Pierrepoint on 28 October 1942.

Twelve

'A PSYCHOPATHIC PERSONALITY'

Newcastle, 1957

Monday, 4 November 1957 was a special day for fifteen-year-old Gordon Lockhart of High Heaton; it was the day he started work at his first job as a porter with Dixon, Blair and Company of Gallowgate, Newcastle, at £2 7s 6d a week. Two weeks later, on Monday 18 November, he started another job, as an apprentice projectionist at the Pavilion cinema in Westgate Road. But during his tea break, at 3.30 p.m. on that very day, he mysteriously disappeared; and when he failed to return home that evening his anxious parents reported their son missing.

For five days the police made enquiries, searched derelict buildings and used tracker dogs to search allotments, but there was no sign of Gordon. There was no known reason for his disappearance, nothing to suggest he would simply go off somewhere. And if his worried parents feared the worst, their feelings would have been intensified when three postcards were delivered, all addressed to Mrs Evelyn Lockhart, Gordon's mother, all sent anonymously and all referring to their son.

The first, received just two days after Gordon's disappearance, read: 'Gordon has gone to London as a woman is after him for money to keep his baby. I will keep you informed about him. G.S.'. The following day the second postcard arrived. It read: 'Gordon is living with prostitutes and he is making money like them. I am not going to write to him any more. I am an old school pal of his, aged seventeen. He borrowed a pound off me to go to London'.

The third postcard, delivered on the Friday, read, simply: 'Gordon is dead'.

There had been widespread publicity about Gordon's disappearance, and his family would have hoped the postcards were the work of a crank, someone who had simply read the newspapers. But a shabbily-dressed man been seen talking to Gordon and hanging around his house, staring into the windows. Who was he? The police made enquiries and

Gordon Lockhart. (Author's collection)

GORDON LOCKHART

decided he could be Albert Edward Matheson, a handyman employed at the St James's Boxing and Wrestling Hall in Strawberry Place, Newcastle. He had 'form' for theft and, perhaps significantly, indecency offences. Clearly the police would have to consider the possibility that he was somehow connected with Gordon's mysterious disappearance – and they did.

Detective Superintendent Robert Davison was the officer leading the hunt for Gordon. On the day the third postcard was received Superintendent Davison, linking Matheson to Gordon's disappearance, ordered a search of his lodgings in Lovaine Place, Newcastle. Matheson had gone by the time the police had identified where he lived, and there was no sign of Gordon.

Police then made a thorough search of the boxing hall, and that Friday evening two detectives found Gordon's mutilated body hidden in a sump underneath the boxing ring. Superintendent Davison's description the murder as 'atrocious' was an understatement; there were twenty-three 'penetrating wounds' in Gordon's scalp and his body had been cut in two.

Police issued a description of Matheson, as well as asking other forces to make 'special enquiries' at boarding houses. He was described as having thin features, bald with a little silver hair on top, several teeth missing, between fifty and sixty and talked with a lisp. A description of his clothing was included. Matheson's name was released to other police forces, though not to the public. Meanwhile, the day after Gordon's body was found, two letters arrived.

In one, to Gordon's parents and bearing an Edinburgh postmark, had been written on the back of a calendar on which there was a picture of a mother and baby: 'Your son was a homosexual maniac. Now it is all over. Was he like this as a baby? The remains are in the

Newcastle ☙ Journal
No. 34,726 SATURDAY NOVEMBER 23 1957 North Mail A KEMSLEY NEWSPAPER 2½d

Atrocious crime, say Newcastle police: 'Sunken cheeks' man sought

BOY IS FOUND MURDERED

River Tyne'. The other, addressed to the Chief Constable of Newcastle City Police, read: 'Have you found that body yet? It is in pieces in the River Tyne in sacks'.

The police were desperate to find Matheson, but a few days later he brought their searching to an end when he walked into a police station in Glasgow and gave himself up. Matheson told Detective Constable Hugh Campbell that when he had left Newcastle he had gone to Edinburgh where he had stayed in the St Andrew's Hotel. He said, 'You will find a pair of shoes in Room 4.' He said he had sent the postcards, and added, 'There is this knife,' indicating a parcel he showed to DC Campbell. He said, 'I struck Lockhart with a claw hammer in the boxing hall. I kept hitting him with it. He was shouting and screaming. I hit him first with a bottle but it broke. I took him downstairs to a well. I left his body there all night. The next day I bought that knife and cut him into two halves.'

Matheson was brought to Newcastle where he appeared before the city magistrates on 25 November, charged with murder. All he had to say was that he wished to apply for legal aid. Two of Gordon's brothers had plenty to say; as Matheson was brought into the courtroom they tried to leap over the dockrail to reach the man accused of murdering their brother. 'With clenched fists and flailing arms,' reported the *Journal and North Mail*, 'the brothers were held back and taken from the courtroom'. At a subsequent hearing, the case took a decidedly different course, when the magistrates were told that Matheson had told police he had taken £35 from Gordon Lockhart: 'I took the money out of his pocket. That's why I killed him.'

Taking money, if he had, made all the difference to the future of Albert Edward Matheson. Giving evidence at that hearing, Detective Chief Inspector James Angus said that on 9 December Matheson had asked to see him, and had said to him:

> I now want to tell you that Lockhart had £35 in a registered envelope in his possession on the Monday, about four o'clock, when he came to the boxing hall. He showed it to me. I asked him for it three times and he would not give it to me. I hit him first with a beer bottle and he still would not give it to me, so I hit him on the head with the hammer. I took the money out of his pocket. That's why I killed him. He got the money off a businessman in Jesmond to post to London.

Hitherto, murder had always been a capital crime, but the Homicide Act of 1957 abolished the death penalty, save in the following circumstances:

Murder committed in the course of or furtherance of theft
Murder by shooting or explosion
Murder whilst resisting arrest or trying to escape
Murder of a police or prison officer
Two murders committed on two separate occasions

Clearly, killing Gordon Lockhart in itself was no longer a capital offence; instead the sentence was a mandatory term of life imprisonment. But stealing money *in the course of murder* was a capital crime; Matheson's immediate future, if convicted, lay in a technicality of the law.

Matheson admitted killing Gordon Lockhart for money. He said his own wages were £4 5s, plus 6s for Saturday night work. 'That's why I knocked the kid off,' he said. 'I brought him in there to get his money.' Other, compelling evidence suggesting that Matheson had had close contact with Gordon Lockhart, included that of Dr J. Ennis, a pathologist, who told the court that a biochemical test showed that a 'sexual offence' had taken place between twenty-four and forty-eight hours before the boy's death. Norman Robert Leigh, of the Forensic Science Laboratory, Gosforth, said the walls in a lavatory at the boxing hall were blood-spattered, indicating a serious attack had occurred.

Thomas Kirkup, of Dixon, Blair and Company at Gallowgate – situated near to St James's Boxing Hall, where Gordon had worked – said that Matheson had recently asked him 'what time Gordon came out'; A fellow lodger of Matheson's, William Black, said he had seen Matheson and Gordon Lockhart together on several occasions. A cleaner at the cinema said that Matheson had asked her if a 'new boy' was starting work there, adding that he was a friend. On Monday 18 November, his first day at the cinema, Gordon went for his tea break at 3.30 and did not return.

Albert Edward Matheson, aged fifty-two, stood trial at Durham Assizes for capital murder on 30 January 1958, before Justice Finnemore. There could be no question that he had killed Gordon Lockhart. Mr Price, prosecuting, told the jury that the killing was 'one of the most ghoulish and sordid crimes it will ever be your misfortune to hear about'.

St James's Boxing and Wrestling Hall in the 1950s. (*Newcastle Evening Chronicle*)

Mr Price said that the day before Gordon Lockhart disappeared Gordon was at home all day, and on that day his mother noticed a man waiting on the other side of the street. 'That man was Matheson,' said Mr Price. He added that the next day, when Gordon went missing, his worried mother waited until after midnight, then reported him missing. 'By that time he had been killed and his body was lying in the St James's Hall,' said Mr Price. A cleaner found Matheson in the Hall early the next morning. The suggestion was that he had been there all night. At eight o'clock on Friday evening a detective found Gordon's body in a sump leading from the passage beneath the boxing hall. 'The body was clothed except for shoes, but was not complete. Parts were found in a bag and other parts had been removed altogether.'

Mr Waller, defending, said the facts were 'largely unchallenged', and that Matheson's defence against a murder conviction lay in Section Two of the Homicide Act, which said that if someone suffered from 'an abnormality of the mind such as to diminish responsibility for his actions, he was guilty of manslaughter'. This defence is valid to this day. Medical evidence, having regard to this, was given by three doctors.

Dr Pickering, Senior Medical Officer at Durham Prison, said Matheson's prison records dated back to 1919. He had spent most of his life in penal institutions or borstal. When he was in prison, he inflicted injury on himself, usually by 'swallowing pieces of razor blades, needles and bits of wire.' Matheson had been a voluntary patient at St Nicholas's mental hospital, Coxlodge, the previous September. At school, he had been described as 'dull and backward'. Because of this he was sent to an industrial school where he was 'noticed to be peculiar, never mixing or playing normally with other boys'. Matheson was too unintelligent for any attempt at psychological treatment. He had threatened suicide.

> He is very egotistical, has never been able to form normal affection and has a detachment from other people. He is obsessed with his sexual perversion. In my opinion he is utterly lacking in moral responsibility. His mental age is less that that of a boy of ten. I formed an opinion that he was one of those unstable individuals who are classed as psychopathic personalities.

Dr Pickering said he believed Matheson would be able to tell whether he was doing wrong, but this was contradicted by two other doctors.

Dr Robert Orton, consultant psychiatrist at Newcastle Infirmary, had examined Matheson in prison. 'He almost enjoyed being interviewed. He would have talked all day.' He was a dull individual with no feeling for anyone else, he said, adding that Matheson had no ability to understand right and wrong. 'On impulse of the moment he tends to do something which pleases him. He suffers from an abnormality of mind. He is without doubt a psychopathic personality, an individual of feeble intelligence.'

Dr Theodore Cuthbert, psychiatrist, said he examined Matheson twice that January and considered he had a development of mind he would have expected of 'someone rather less than ten'. 'He simply has not grown up,' said Dr Cuthbert. 'He is childish, shallow and

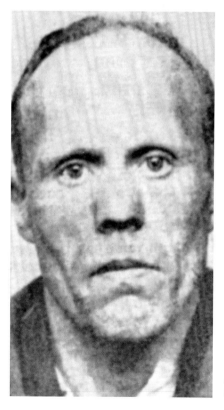

Albert Edward Matheson. He was described by Lord Goddard as 'a monster'. (Author's collection)

immature emotionally. I don't think he has developed anything like a normal sense of right or wrong.'

Mr Waller said Matheson was not insane 'in the normal sense', 'but the abnormality of mind was such as to diminish his responsibility for what he had done and that therefore he was not liable to be convicted of murder but of manslaughter.' Not guilty of murder, on the grounds of diminished responsibility, was Matheson's defence. The jury rejected it, taking sixty-five minutes to return a verdict of capital murder; twelve men good and true would have had little consideration for what they would perceive as fancy words, considering instead the brutal killing of an innocent young lad by a maniac, as Matheson would later be called. Wearing the customary black cap, Justice Finnemore told Matheson, 'You have been found guilty of the gravest crime of capital murder. There is only one punishment and that is that you should suffer death according to the law.'

Matheson's appeal was heard before five judges, including the Lord Chief Justice, Lord Goddard, on the basis that the medical evidence given at the trial had been unchallenged and disregarded. Lord Goddard said:

> It is the most horrible case I have come across in my experience. He [Matheson] is a monster. There is no other word for it. The revolting nature of the crime would cause most people to say that it was the work of a maniac resembling, as it did, the murders which terrorised the East End of London, known as the Ripper murders.

His lordship said that one could understand the feeling of revulsion among the jury in returning their verdict, feeling that 'such a creature should not live'. 'But,' he added, 'what were the feelings which justified the jury returning their verdict contrary to unchallenged medical evidence?' He referred the case to the Court of Criminal Appeal, which passed judgement the next day, in Matheson's presence, that the verdict of the jury was 'unreasonable'. A conviction of manslaughter on the grounds of diminished responsibility

was returned, and Matheson was sentenced to twenty years' imprisonment. He heard the verdict 'showing no emotion whatsoever'.

The rules under the Homicide Act, requiring that murder had to be committed 'in the course of or furtherance of theft' to make it a capital offence, made the law look an ass. The theft of £35 was the focus of the prosecution case, in order to return a verdict of capital murder. The issue of money took priority over the dreadful crime itself: a sexual assault or assaults, a brutal attack and subsequent mutilation and secretion of the body. This law lasted only a handful of years before being removed from the statute book. As for Matheson, he was later certified as insane and never released.

BIBLIOGRAPHY

BOOKS

Ellis, John *Diary of a Hangman* (Forum Press, 1997)
Redfern, Barry *The Shadow of the Gallows* (Tyne Bridge Publishing, 2003)

NEWSPAPERS AND PERIODICALS

Alnwick and County Gazette
Alnwick Mercury
Belington News Post Leader
Berwick Advertiser
Berwick Journal
Hexham Courant
Morpeth Herald and Reporter
Newcastle Guardian
Newcastle Evening Chronicle
Newcastle Journal
Newcastle Journal and North Mail
Shields Daily News

Other titles published by The History Press

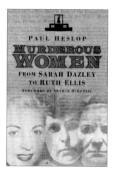

Murderous Women: From Sarah Dazley to Ruth Ellis
PAUL HESLOP

Serial poisoners, crimes of passion, brutal slayings and infanticide; this new book examines the stories and subsequent trials behind the most infamous cases of British female killers between the early part of the nineteenth century and the 1950s. Among the cases featured here is that of Sarah Dazley, hanged in 1843 for poisoning her second husband; Mary Ann Cotton, who murdered up to twenty-one people, including many members of her own family and Amelia Dyer, the 'baby farmer' who murdered countless numbers of children.

978 0 7509 5081 7

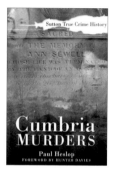

Cumbria Murders
PAUL HESLOP

Cumbria Murders brings together numerous murderous tales that shocked not only the county but also made headlines throughout the country. They include the cases of Wai Sheung Siu Miao, strangled while on honeymoon in 1928; William Armstrong, shot by the Revd Joseph Smith in 1851; Ann Sewell, stabbed to death by farmhand George Cass in 1860; and the murder of Jack West at his home near Workington in 1964, whose killers were the last two men to be lawfully hanged in England.

978 0 7509 4748 0

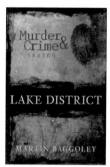

Murder & Crime: Lake District
MARTIN BAGGOLEY

Drawing on a wide selection of sources and illustrated with more than sixty photographs, this collection of grisly tales explores the darker side of the Lake District's past. It features the tale of the 'Keswick Imposter' and the account of an eighteenth-century gang who repeatedly tried to kidnap a wealthy (but alcoholic) landowner and marry him to a prostitute in order to lay their hands on his fortune.

978 0 7524 4805 3

Haunted Northumberland
DARREN W. RITSON

This fascinating book contains a terrifying collection of true-life, spine-chilling tales from across Northumberland. Featuring stories of unexplained phenomena, apparitions and poltergeists, and including the tale of the Hexham Heads, the Pink Lady of Bamburgh Castle and the ghost of Hadrian's Wall, this book is guaranteed to make your blood run cold.

978 0 7524 5861 8

Visit our website and discover thousands of other History Press books.

www.thehistorypress.co.uk